COUNSELING AFRICAN AMERICAN FAMILIES

Edited by
Jo-Ann Lipford Sanders and Carla Bradley

THE FAMILY PSYCHOLOGY AND COUNSELING SERIES

■ ■ ■

Developed Collaboratively by the American Counseling Association and
the International Association of Marriage and Family Counselors

COUNSELING AFRICAN AMERICAN FAMILIES

10 9 8 7 6 5 4 3 2 1

American Counseling Association
5999 Stevenson Avenue
Alexandria, VA 22304

Director of Publications
Carolyn C. Baker

Production Manager
Bonny E. Gaston

Copy Editor
Lucy Blanton

Cover design by Martha Woolsey

Library of Congress Cataloging-in-Publication Data

Counseling African American families / edited by Jo-Ann Lipford
   Sanders and Carla Bradley
      p. cm. (The family psychology and counseling series)
   Includes bibliographical references.
   ISBN 1-55620-221-0 (alk. paper)
      1. African Americans—Counseling of. 2. African Americans—
Mental health. 3. African American families. 4. Family psycho-
therapy. I. Lipford Sanders, Jo-Ann. II. Bradley, Carla. III. Series.

RC451.5.N4 C68 2001
616.89'156'08996073—dc21

                                                                    2001045887

The Family Psychology and Counseling Series

Transitioning From Individual to Family Counseling
Charles Huber, PhD

Understanding Stepfamilies: Implications for Assessment and Treatment
Debra Huntley, PhD

In Preparation

Practical Approaches for School Counselors: Integrating Family Counseling in School Settings
Lynn D. Miller, PhD

Advisory Board

■ ■ ■

THE FAMILY PSYCHOLOGY AND COUNSELING SERIES

Table of Contents

From the Series Editor

Counseling African American Families discusses important issues in the clinical assessment of African American families. A major challenge confronting today's counseling profession is meeting the therapeutic needs of clients from diverse cultures. The Association for Multicultural Counseling and Development (AMCD) has helped by developing a series of multicultural competencies. These involve further understanding and conceptualization of treatment for African American families as well as for those from other distinct cultures.

Each culture has had unique experiences with the American culture. Those members of African American families, with a history of racism and discrimination, have developed what Nancy Boyd-Franklin (1989) has described as "healthy cultural suspicion." This suspicion is often the first response clinicians encounter when working with Black families. This suspicion is often viewed as resistance; however, when we understand the multigenerational experiences with racism, rejection, and the intrusion of dominate society, this response certainly makes clear sense. Therapists need to help these families learn to be empowered. This can happen when we understand the cultural diversity in Black families and use their cultural strengths in therapy. The cultural strengths of African Americans include roles played by extended family members; the common practice of informal adoption; the desire of an education for their children, regardless of their feelings about the school system; love for other children and the desire to be good parents; and survival skills (Boyd-Franklin, 1989). This monograph understands these principles and addresses issues that are essential for work with African American families, such as the role of Black men, parenting, and Black churches. The strength of this monograph, however, is in the way the African American family is understood and how counseling strategies and implications are developed. Sanders and Bradley have pulled together the leading spokespeople in the understanding and treatment of African American families. This monograph provides the necessary information for effectively meeting the complex needs of African American families.

—Jon Carlson, PsyD, EdD
Series Editor

Reference

Boyd-Franklin, N. (1989). *Black families in counseling therapy*. New York: Guilford Press.

■ ■ ■

Preface

A major challenge confronting the counseling profession at the beginning of the 21st century is meeting the therapeutic needs of African American families. Although the counseling literature has seen a proliferation of writings and research regarding multicultural counseling, little discussion or information is available on the strengths and breadth of issues that impact African American parents and their children. Much of what is available to counselors is contained in the education and psychological literature in which the prevailing notion is that African American parents are incompetent, irresponsible, and pathological. Moreover, a 2001 research of journals and other periodicals published by the American Counseling Association turned up few articles and virtually no books or handbooks on the psychological assessment and experiences of African American families.

This apparent void in the counseling literature is of particular concern given the increasing numbers of African American families that are being served by family and mental health counselors. The current silence within the counseling profession regarding the needs of African American families reinforces the stereotypical and deficit-ridden information that has been presented to counselors and counselor trainees in past decades.

Hence, the primary purpose of this monograph is to present a well-balanced discussion of the issues involved in the clinical assessment and treatment of African American families. More specifically, the authors explore the common and distinct experiences of African American families as they navigate through a society that is often hostile and racist toward them. The chapters illuminate ways for understanding these unique circumstances and explain culturally responsive interventions that address such counseling concerns.

It is important to consider, however, that before concepts or strategies presented in this monograph are used with clients, counselors must have or receive training in the fundamental principles of multicultural counseling. The Association for Multicultural Counseling and Development (AMCD) has recommended specific multicultural competencies for counselors working with clients from culturally diverse backgrounds (Arredondo et al., 1996). Among the AMCD suggestions is that counselors have specific knowledge about their own racial and cultural backgrounds and how their personal backgrounds affect their definitions and bias of normality/abnormality and the process of counseling. Also recommended is that counselors establish alliances with counselors from backgrounds different from their own and maintain a dialogue with them regarding multicultural differences and preferences. Additionally noteworthy is that this monograph restricts its focus to African Americans or Black people who have lived the majority of their lives in the United States. Although identification labels have been an aspect of contention and much debate both within and outside Black communities, this monograph uses the identification labels *African American* and *Black* interchangeably. Counselors are best served when they inquire how a client self-identifies. We acknowledge that by not including chapters on recent African immigrant populations or Latino groups of African descent this monograph is not exhaustive in its coverage.

Efforts were made to include in this monograph the viewpoints of trained counseling professionals and voices of grassroot helpers to whom African American families traditionally go for assistance. In no way did the contributors or we seek for a consensus of opinions or thoughts. Each was encouraged to give "voice" to their respective subject areas. Counseling implications and strategies are offered in each chapter.

Often in our classes students state, "just show me what to do" to work effectively with African American families. Our answer is summarized in the phrase, "Think, Hear, and Know Them." In most instances students are uncomfortable that there is no one model to use with this population and that there are instead several areas that counselors need to be aware of when working with African Americans. One of these is heterogeneity against the "myth of sameness." Although linked by a common bond of historical oppression, the internalization of racism, classism, and other forms of discrimination experiences differs within this group. A second—in part due to an "ethos of blame" and a quest for individual control and responsibility—is that the legacy of slavery and, more significantly, its residual effects in the everyday lives of Black people, are often minimized or overlooked. A third area counselors need to be aware of is the assumed universality of experiences as evidenced in counseling training programs.

Part I of this monograph focuses on family structures. In chapter 1, Mary Smith Arnold sets the stage to see and hear African American families on a postmodernist stage. She introduces and defines the historical evolution of family structures and, most specifically, the changes these structures now face as a result of the postmodern era. She suggests that fragmentation and the dismissal of essentialism cannot overshadow the universal truth of race consciousness for many African American families.

Chapter 2, written by three African American fathers, Sylvester Huston, Terry D. Lipford, and Jeffrey Smith, gives voice to the concern and presence of many fathers in Black families. While not denying the large numbers of female-headed families, these three fathers evince their contribution to the home. The chapter suggests the possibility of movement from a peripheral perspective to a centripetal focus, and ends with a narrative description of one father's joys and trials in the rearing of Black sons.

Part II focuses on parenting concerns, including styles, disċipline, and socialization. Chapter 3, by Carla Bradley, explores various responsive parenting styles. She offers insights about discipline styles and specifically addresses the myth that African American parents are monolithic in discipline patterns. She concludes the chapter by addressing questions commonly asked by African American parents. Chapter 4, by Jo-Ann Lipford Sanders, outlines various parental attitudes and themes relating to racial socialization for African American children. She states that racial socialization may be used as an intervention strategy in the development of a healthy self-concept for Black children.

Part III focuses on indigenous social supports, on the voices of traditional givers and helpers within many African American communities. Paul Hill, Jr., in chapter 5, offers understanding of the use of rites of passage programs in the development of a healthy self-concept for Black people. He provides a step-by-step design of a rites of passage program. Chapter 6, by Rufus G. W. Sanders, considers the role that the Black church has played in the lives of African American families. Putting the church in its historical context, he traces the influence of spirituality and religion on the social structures of Black people since American slavery.

Part IV pulls things together. Chapter 7 uses the strengths model suggested throughout the monograph to offer specific implications and strategies to use with this population.

We believe that although this monograph is not comprehensive, it is timely, and an important step in creating a genuine understanding of the unique needs of African Americans and their families.

—*Jo-Ann Lipford Sanders, PhD, and*
Carla Bradley, PhD

Reference

Arredondo, P., Toporek, R., Brown, S. P., Jones, J., Locke, D. C., Sanchez, J., & Stadler, H. (1996, January). *Operationalization of the multicultural counseling competencies.* Alexandria, VA: Association for Multicultural Counseling and Development, American Counseling Association.

■ ■ ■

Biographies

Jo-Ann Lipford Sanders, PhD, is an assistant professor in the counseling department at Heidelberg College in Tiffin, Ohio. Dr. Lipford Sanders is a member of the editorial boards of *The Family Journal* and the *Journal of Counseling & Development*. She has had several leadership positions in the American Counseling Association, including chair of the ACA Ethics Committee. Her research interests include African American female adolescent development, African and African American women, and African American families. Dr. Lipford Sanders is a Licensed Professional Clinical Counselor.

Carla Bradley, PhD, is an associate professor at the University of North Carolina at Charlotte in the Department of Counseling, Special Education, and Child Development. She is a member of the editorial board of *The Family Journal*. Dr. Bradley has held leadership roles in state and national counseling organizations. She has researched and published in the areas of counselor training and supervision, multicultural counseling, and child-rearing practices. Her research interests are in the areas of counselor competence and training, child discipline, and socialization practices. Dr. Bradley has 10 years of experience working with African American families, and is a Licensed Professional Clinical Counselor.

Jon Carlson, PsyD, EdD, is distinguished professor at Governors State University in University Park, Illinois, and director of the Lake Geneva Wellness Clinic in Wisconsin. He is the founding editor of *The Family Journal: Counseling and Therapy for Couples and Families* and has served as president of the International Association of Marriage and Family Counselors. Dr. Carlson holds a diplomate in family psychology from the American Board of Professional Psychology. He is a fellow of the American Psychological Association and a certified sex therapist by the American Association of Sex Educators, Counselors, and Therapists. He has authored more than 25 books and 125 professional articles. He has received numerous awards for his professional contributions from major professional organizations, including the American Counseling Association, the Association for Counselor Education and Supervision, and the American Psychological Association. Dr. Carlson and his spouse of 32 years, Laura, are the parents of five children and grandparents of two.

Contributors

Mary Smith Arnold, PhD, is university professor in the Division of Psychology and Counseling at Governors State University in University Park, Illinois. Her research and practice has focused on African American families and enhancing counselor effectiveness across multicultural differences.

Paul Hill, Jr., MA, is a licensed social worker; the executive director of the East End Neighborhood House in Cleveland, Ohio; and founder of the National Rites of Passage Institute. He and his wife are the parents of seven children.

Sylvester Huston, MA, is a doctoral student at Kent State University in Kent, Ohio. He is also a professor of respiratory therapy at Stark State College in North Canton, Ohio, and currently in private clinical practice. He and Doris are the parents of one child.

Terry D. Lipford, MA, is the principal of Central Primary School in Bedford, Ohio. His research interest is early childhood development. He and Phyllis are the parents of three children.

Rufus G. W. Sanders, PhD, is the senior minister at the Emmanuel Temple Church in Sandusky, Ohio. His writings on race and culture appear in newspapers in Ohio and Texas.

Jeffrey Smith, PhD, is an assistant professor of counseling at Creighton University, Omaha, Nebraska. He has published in the area of social anxiety and counseling issues affecting male development. He and Lillie are the parents of three children.

PART

FAMILY
STRUCTURES

1

African American Families in the Postmodern Era

Mary Smith Arnold, PhD

The postmodern era is marked by incessant rapid economic and social transformations. Family relationships, in general, are being transformed as a result of massive changes in labor markets, roles within the family, relaxed sexual standards, new technologies, and many more alterations in private and public conventions. African American families have not been impervious to these large-scale societal changes. This period of societal transition represents a new set of challenges for African American families.

African American families have historically been resourceful and adaptive in response to the many social forces that have impacted their existence. Billingsley (1968, 1992) called our attention to the unique features and resilience of Black families. He also pointed out the tendency on the part of social scientists to underestimate and distort the viability of African American families. It is imperative, in light of the current national debate on family values, and the continued negative attitudes regarding Black families, that counselors gain an understanding of African American families.

This chapter reviews the historical and contemporary context of African American families so counselors may gain a fuller picture of such families. Attention is also given to two elements of the postmodern era that pose particular challenges to African American families: fragmentation and the dismissal of essentialism. Suggestions for counselors are offered to assist with identifying the concerns of families grappling with the challenges posed by the current era.

Postmodern Era and Theory

The conditions that mark the postmodern era are economic globalization, an explosion in information and communication technologies, global labor markets, and global consumer markets. These processes create rapidly occurring changes that affect individuals and family life. West (1997) stated that the consequences of these changes for our society are severe.

> The precious systems of caring and nurturing are eroding. Market moralities and mentalities, fueled by economic imperatives to make a profit at nearly any cost, yield unprecedented levels of loneliness, isolation, and sadness. And our public life lies in shambles, shot through with icy cynicism and paralyzing pessimism....This bleak portrait is accentuated in Black America. The fragile middle class... fights a White backlash. The devastated Black working class fears further underemployment or unemployment. And the besieged Black poor struggle to survive. (p. xi)

The urgency in these words by Cornel West resonates in the lives of many American families even as they rush to fill the void with the latest consumer craze.

Postmodernism, as a social theory, is about the way the world is changing because of these sweeping political, economic, and technological transformations. It developed in response to modernism, a period in the history of western social thought that attempted to explain all of human behavior by asserting a single cause. Marxism (class distinctions), psychoanalysis (ego satisfaction), and feminism (patriarchy) are examples of modernist theories that posited universal truths regarding human behavior.

Postmodern theory is characterized by "the notion that there may no longer be any universally accepted truths, even within a single culture..." (Lewis, 1993, p. 337). An idea central to postmodernism is *fragmentation*. Postmodernists argue that categories such as *man* or *woman* are too fragmented by race/ethnicity, class, sexual orientation, religion, geographical differences, and personal experiences to have any real meaning. Gergen (1991), a postmodernist social psychologist, attributed this fragmentation to social saturation.

Emerging technologies saturate us with the voices of humankind, both harmonious and alien. As we absorb their varied rhymes and reasons, they become part of us and we of them. Social saturation furnishes us with a multiplicity of incoherent and unrelated languages of the self.

For everything we "know to be true" about ourselves, other voices within respond with doubt and even derision. This fragmentation of self-conceptions corresponds to a multiplicity of incoherent and disconnected relationships...

The fully saturated self becomes no self at all. (pp. 6–7)

It follows then, that regarding race postmodernists take the position that differences within groups are so great that distinctions growing from the racial categories of Black and White are meaningless (Walby, 1992). They repudiate the idea of a cultural essence and dismiss racism as an outcome rooted in class differences rather than a universal experience for Black people.

Although it is likely that aspects of social saturation and fragmentation are impacting African American families, they must still contend with their universal truth since arriving on these shores of the persistent and pernicious effects of racism on family life. The postmodern era does not differ from previous times in that sense for Black families. White and Rogers (2000), in their review of economic circumstances for all families the 1990s, found "persistent racial inequalities in economic opportunities" for African Americans and Hispanics. However, some scholars have suggested that "economic position" rather than race has become the most salient factor in African American life (Wilson, 1980). It is important that family counselors not deny or diminish the truth of the Black experience, albeit varied and diverse, which is that racism has an effect on family life.

Essentialism

The other side of the fragmentation coin is *essentialism*. This represents the idea that concepts such as man and woman do, in fact, have essential or common qualities that distinguish them from one another. Essentialism has been characterized as constructing and presenting identity as "monolithic," "homogeneous," and in an "exclusionary way" (hooks, 1994). Postmodernists refute this tendency to claim one essence for an entire group. For instance, statements such as "all men are..." or "all women do..." or "all Black people say..." ignore the differences among men, women, and Black people based on, for example, class, sexual orientation, religion, disabilities, and geographical location that mitigate against a common essence that all people in any one group share. Essentialism has been said to lead to an us-versus-them discourse and is associated with modernism.

Scholars have repeatedly found that African American families share core values across class lines (Billingsley, 1968, 1992; Hill, 1971, 1998; Mosley-Howard & Evans, 2000). Scholars have often debated whether these core values stem from the African heritage of Black people or their common experience with race oppression. Deciding on the origin of these values is irrelevant to our discussion in this chapter. It is important to note, however, that the strengths Hill (1971) identified 30 years ago continue to appear as thematic influences in the lives of contemporary African American families.

Mosley-Howard and Evans (2000) studied relationships and experiences of diverse African American families. Their ethnographic examination revealed six themes: (a) reliance on and transmission of tradition, (b) pride in cultural heritage, (c) overt teaching about racism, (d) negotiation between two cultures, (e) a belief in education, and (f) spirituality and the church. Other researchers have found similar themes, such as valuing extended kinship (Johnson, 1999) and community (Gaines, 1997). These data clearly speak to a cultural pattern among African American families that is positive and generative, and that fosters successful development. These findings stand in contradiction to the postmodernist assertion that there is no common essence within cultural groups such as African Americans. It also suggests that African American families are substantively different from White families.

Historical Context

Families have historically been the most significant social and political unit in African societies. When Europeans arrived on the African continent, they found highly developed civilizations that were thousands of years old. Families formed the economic and religious foundation of these civilizations. They had laws and mores about social behavior, suitable marriage partners, transference of wealth and power, and interactions between separate tribal communities. Billingsley (1992) listed several features of African families that have survived in African American families. They include (a) the primacy of blood ties rather than ties of marriage, (b) the importance of the extended family, (c) strong valuing of children and respect for the elderly, and (d) role reciprocity.

These features are not to be viewed as standards that all African American families adhere to or implement but rather as underlying values with varying degrees of saliency within families. To recognize the cultural threads woven into the fabric of African American family life is not the same as saying that there is a single Black family type. African American families are heterogeneous reflecting all of the diversity related to class, religion, sexual orientation, geographical location, and family composition.

However, it is important that family counselors understand that the Black family began in Africa and not in Europe or the United States. Any expectation that African American families will uniformly mirror families of European heritage is a gross misconception. Yet it is also true that Africans adapted in order to survive in America and created a unique and complex institution—the African American family. The Black family has been a central part of the mosaic of American family life from the earliest beginnings of this nation. Africans arrived on these shores as explorers in the 1500s, as indentured servants in 1619, and later as captives held in forced servitude for 250 years (Franklin, 1974).

Africans had to reconstitute themselves into families after the devastation of savage kidnappings, the Middle Passage, and enslavement. The African slave trade and the institution of slavery ruptured families, tribal connections, and left indelible scars on the African continent as well as among those who were ripped from its shores. Yet the Black family reconfigured itself under the most hostile and alienating conditions to sustain the endurance of a people (Berlin & Rowland, 1997).

One of the greatest injustices of slavery was the denial that Africans possessed the capacity to love or maintain familial bonds. Slaves were objects of commercial value and property. Social mores held, in addition, that slaves were animals such as mules or other beasts of burden. Therefore, to acknowledge familial ties would be to accord to slaves a degree of humanity that was not institutionally supported by society. Countless disruptions to family life were caused by selling family members away from one another, selecting males and females to serve as breeders, regardless of bonds of prior intimacy, and the practice of slave owners taking Black women as concubines. However, even within the brutal constraints of slavery Black men and women developed loving relationships and nourished family ties (Berlin & Rowland, 1997; Gutman, 1976).

With the passage of the Thirteenth Amendment to the U.S. Constitution on December 6, 1865, abolishing slavery, Black people were legally able to construct families. Even though they had secured the right as free men and women to marry and to retain their children, it was widely believed that Black people were lacking in intelligence and that their families would be inherently inferior and pathological (Berlin & Rowland, 1997; Gutman, 1996). Almost 150 years after the Civil War and the end of slavery, similar attitudes about Black people and Black families still prevail.

In spite of the negative environment, the structural inequalities, and daily brutalities that Black people faced, whether in northern or southern states, they worked, nurtured their children, and built vibrant communities. They formed self-help societies, created financial institutions, hospitals, churches, and colleges and universities. They fought in every major war, always distinguishing themselves with valor. African American families survived the harsh discrimination of the Jim Crow laws, the Great Depression, the migration north, urbanization, the New Deal, the Civil Rights Movement, the War on Poverty, and economic recessions. During every period of struggle that occurred for American families, African Americans were also affected and made significant contributions to the general welfare of the country. However, their contributions were seldom appreciated or acknowledged.

Contemporary Context

There are 35.1 million African Americans in the United States. Of this number 5.2 million are classified as Hispanic Blacks. This represents 13% of the total U.S. population. There are 8.4 million Black families (U.S. Census Bureau, 2000). The U.S. Census Bureau defines a family as "two or more persons living together and related by blood, marriage, or adoptions" (Schwartz & Scott, 1994). This definition favors married couples with children. It tacitly suggests that all other family forms are the exception to the nuclear family model.

In contrast, many scholars have defined the African American family as a "constellation of households related by blood or marriage or function that provides basic instrumental and expressive functions of the family to members of those networks" (Hill, 1998, p. 1). Individuals, or nonrelated fictive kin, who fulfill important family functions are also considered family members. This discrepancy in how family is experienced and defined by African Americans versus the definition of agencies that represent the dominant society often leads to inaccurate and underinformed perspectives on African American families. African American families are portrayed in the media as crisis ridden with multiple problems and as a perpetual drain on society's resources. In general, scholarly treatments of Black families have done little to alter this perspective. The counseling literature often reflects this same pattern. The treatment focus, and hence the problem orientation, of the counseling literature seldom allows for a look at the broader circumstances of Black families. Hill (1998) pointed out that the focus of social scientists has been "on the minority (16%) of families who are female-headed, poor, and on welfare, and depicts them as representing the majority of Black families." This unbalanced, deficit-oriented approach obscures the broader picture and creates "narrow, flat images" of African American family life (Arnold, 1994). For instance, more than two-thirds of African Americans are not poor. Among married couples, which make up 47% of all Black families, 80% have incomes above $25,000 a year. The data further reflect that 13.3% of families have an income range of $25,000 to $34,999; 18% a range of $35,000 to $49,999; 25.2% a range of $50,000 to $74,999; and 22.6% a range of $75,000 and over. There is virtually no difference in the percentage of middle-income married couples earning $35,000 to $74,999 between Blacks (43.2%) and Whites (42.3%; U.S. Census Bureau, 2000). Married couples enjoy a larger income because of the presence of two wage earners in the home. White and Rogers (2000) found two wage earners to be normative among American families. They found that "among couples in which the husband was employed, wives were also employed in 61% of Hispanic, 79% of African American, and 75% of White couples in 1994."

It is at the highest and lowest levels of the income scale that a real gap occurs. The percentage of African American families earning $75,000 or more is 22%. There is a 10 point percentage gap with 32.9% of Whites earning $75,000 or more. At the lowest end of the income scale 20.8% of Black couples earn less than $25,000 and 14.1% of White couples (U.S. Census Bureau, 2000). Furthermore, White and Rogers (2000) pointed out that during the 1990s growth in earnings occurred for people at the top and actually declined for people at the lower end of the scale. Also, people in the top 5% of the income scale made the greatest gains.

According to census data in 1998, there were 34.5 million people in poverty, including 9.1 million Blacks and 15.8 million Whites. Although there are almost two times as many Whites that are poor, a larger share of the Black population is poor at 26% in contrast to 8% for Whites. Therefore, Black people are three times more likely than Whites to be among the people in poverty. A total of 7.2 million families lived in poverty in 1998. The U.S. Census Bureau has defined the poverty threshold for a family of four as $16,600. Of families living in poverty in 1998, 2.0 million were African American and 3.3 million were White. Again, the numbers represent 23% of all African American families and only 6% of all White families (U.S. Census Bureau, 2000).

In the foreground in the American picture of Black families have been those families at the lowest end of the income scale, the 26% of all Black people who live in poverty. This rate is double the 13% poverty rate for the total U.S. population (U.S. Census Bureau, 2000). An alarming number of this population is comprised of women and children. Among this population, called the "poorest of the poor" or the "underclass" (Wilson, 1980), 66.8% are African American female householders who earn less than $25,000 and 46% are White female householders. The stereotypical image of this population is that of young, never-married, and welfare dependent; however, this segment of the population is comprised of widowed, divorced, separated, and never-married women, many of whom are among the working poor. Among male householders a similar disproportionate ratio exists at 43.1% and 26.2% for Black and White men, respectively, who earned less than $25,000 (U.S. Census Bureau, 2000).

Additionally, the poverty rates for children, the elderly, and men reflect the same pattern of African Americans being three to four times more likely to live in poverty. Of all children under the age of 18 in 1998, 19% lived in poverty, but 37% of Black children—in contrast to 11% of White children—lived in poverty. For people 65 years old and over, 10% lived in poverty in 1998; however, three times as many Black elderly than White elderly lived in poverty at rates of 26% and 8% respectively. Approximately 11% of all men were below the poverty line in 1998. Again, the rate of poverty for Black men was three times greater at 23% in contrast to 7% for White men. For elderly men, the contrast is even greater, with rates four times as high for Black men (21%) than for White men (5%; U.S. Census Bureau, 2000).

An extensive review by White and Rogers (2000) of economic circumstances and outcomes for American families revealed persistent racial inequalities in economic opportunities for African Americans and Hispanics. They also noted that African Americans and Hispanics experience unemployment at rates of two to three times higher than Whites. These findings are reminiscent of an old saying about Blacks in the job market, "last hired, first fired." Broman (1997), in a discussion of how unemployment affects individuals and families, noted that job loss created an increase in family tension and stress. He also indicated that African Americans experienced longer periods of unemployment after job loss.

The implications of these census data and research findings suggest the presence of structural economic inequality at the societal level. Carmichael and Hamilton identified structural barriers to economic opportunities and political equality as institutional racism whether they were intentionally designed to be so or not (cited in Hill, 1998). Institutional racism is not confined to the labor market. It is systemic and touches every area of social and economic life.

Hill (1998) discussed the impact of structural discrimination on Black families. Structural discrimination is a form of institutional racism that is not consciously or intentionally racist; yet in its effect it discriminates against Black people. One example Hill pointed to is the policy change created in 1983 by the 98th Congress in order to strengthen the Social Security Trust Fund. The age for full benefits at retirement was changed from 62 to 67 years old for people born in 1960 and later. The negative effects of this change on Black men and their families is stunning because the life expectancy of Black men is less than 65 years of age. The life expectancy of White men is 7 years greater at 72 years old. The life expectancy of Black women is also greater than that of Black men. This means that many Black men will not live long enough to receive full benefits. It also means, for those who retire early at reduced benefits, that their surviving spouses will have to live their remaining years with permanently reduced benefits.

There are countless examples of structural discrimination as well as intentional forms of institutional racism that affect African American families. Examples of structural discrimination that family counselors might examine for their negative impact on African American families are (a) zero-tolerance school policies, (b) foster care policies and regulations that exclude relatives from receiving important benefits, and (c) dual arrest laws in domestic violence cases.

Challenges of the Postmodern Era

In addition to the structural inequalities that may be direct or indirect manifestations of racism, African American families are also grappling with the current social forces of the postmodern era that seem to occur at the speed of light. The features of African families that survived in America that Billingsley (1992) identified, and the strengths of Black families identified by Hill (1971), have been viewed as indicators of well-functioning, healthy African American families. Signs of the times that have a particularly deleterious impact on Black families are the growing numbers of children in foster care, the dispersal of extended family members, and fluid and changing standards of child rearing. Each of these outcomes may surface in the concerns of clients regarding the function of family members. They are not the total universe of problems besetting Black families due to the current times, but they represent areas of vulnerability for Black families.

An indicator of the degree of stress of many Black families is the growing number of children in foster care. One of the strongest values of African American families is the primacy of blood ties; it is under severe strain from current social forces. Black children are two times as likely to be in foster care, and they are more likely to be in foster care because of child neglect issues, such as inadequate supervision and malnutrition. Black children are also more likely to be in prolonged foster care. According to researchers the prolonged care is associated with greater developmental risks (Taylor, Tucker, Chatters, & Jayakody, 1997). Family counselors must pay close attention to these children and their caregivers. There may be deep layers of anger and despair among family members who feel trapped by the obligation to care for relatives. And at the very least, issues of abandonment and anger may be prominent with children in foster care.

Other effects of the times are changes in the kinship networks of African American families. The processes associated with social mobility, with differences in educational and job opportunities, create disparities in resources among members of the extended family. People may in fact share resources with those who have fewer means in their families, but social distance can create emotional dissonance. Another consequence of social mobility has been the dispersal of family members into many regions of the country. Young people often relocate to attend college and then seek employment far from home. The vitality of youth that could be utilized by the extended family to care for younger children and elderly family members is no longer available. Recent data have shown that the size of the extended family network has been reduced and that the functions of the extended family may be changing. Johnson (1999) reported on a study conducted by Jayakody, Chatters, and Taylor indicating that single mothers received from extended family members less instrumental support in the form of money and childcare but greater emotional support. This is in contrast to earlier studies that reported on the availability of robust extended family networks.

The most disturbing change in Black families from the perspective of many adults is the discrepancy between child-rearing practices today versus those of past generations. A resounding theme among adults across class lines and generations is how the youth of today have such different values. Of course, across ethnic groups and classes the theme of young people as out of control and strange is as old as the human family itself. However, African Americans' standards for child rearing seem to be in conflict with the current mores of society. Therefore, there is greater uncertainty about how to best rear children (see chapters 3 and 4). This often leads to greater intergenerational stress within families. Also, with the erosion of communities, parents in low-income and middle-income neighborhoods feel they have fewer adults to assist with the "upbringing" of their children (Mosley-Howard & Evans, 2000).

Counseling Practice

It is critical that counselors heed the messages of this chapter in their work with African American families. The first message is that African American families are not reflections of White families that hold primarily European values. The second is that African American families are more complex and diverse in their function and structure than the current popular images suggest. A third is that racism affects African American families, but that they nevertheless remain the most important unit for fulfilling the needs of their members. Given the circumstances presented in this chapter, how can family counselors best assist African American families that are struggling with the challenges of the postmodern era? By:

- Interrogating their own thinking and attitudes about such families. This is critical regardless of the race/ethnicity of the counselor. Where bias, prejudice, and a lack of knowledge reveal themselves within the counselor, an obligation exists to change them.
- Openly speaking to clients about the challenges they face regarding racism. Ask for their help in understanding the impact of race in their lives. Again, the counselor should do this irrespective of his or her race/ethnicity.
- Learning more about the effects of institutional racism and other forms of oppression on families, especially about the

racism growing from social service systems that counselors often feel compelled to support.

- Respecting the experiences of families grappling with racism. Do not offer alternative realities or stories that deny or dilute the truth of the impact of racism on family members.
- Offering families a balanced picture of the current conditions that affect family life as well as emphasizing the resilience and adaptive powers of Black families.

These strategies are offered to counselors to assist with reconstructing their view of African American families. It is the hope and goal of this chapter that counselors may resist the dominant pejorative messages that say African American families are inherently dysfunctional and inferior.

Conclusion

Most people do not identify the changes they are experiencing as having anything to with the postmodern era, but there are echoes of postmodern themes in almost every conversation with adults, especially parents. These discussions appear often to be charged with grief and fear for African Americans. Characteristic of the postmodern era are a sense of loss, fears of what might come next, and anxiety that the other shoe will soon fall. Historian Stephanie Coontz (1997) and sociologists Mary Schwartz and Barbara Scott (1994) have advised, however, that we take the long view of family life. Examining current trends in light of 19th century challenges demonstrates and clarifies that although the African American family is facing many difficulties they have also met and overcome similar challenges. Today is unquestionably a period of stress and uncertainty, yet the African American family remains viable and will likely remain so even as it evolves into the future. Family counselors can play a very important role in restoring balance to the picture of African American family life with our clients, other professionals, and the public.

References

Arnold, M. S. (1994). Exploding the myths: African American families at promise. In S. Lubbeck & E. Swadener (Eds.), *Children and families at promise*. Albany: State University of New York Press.

Berlin, I., & Rowland, L. S. (Eds.). (1997). *Families and freedom: A documentary history of African American kinship in the Civil War era.* New York: New Press.

Billingsley, A. (1968). *Black families in White America.* Englewood Cliffs, NJ: Prentice Hall.

Billingsley, A. (1992). *Climbing Jacob's ladder: The enduring legacy of African American families.* New York: Simon & Schuster.

Broman, C. L. (1997). Families, unemployment, and well-being. In R. J. Taylor, J. S. Jackson, & L. M. Chatters (Eds.), *Family life in Black America* (pp. 157–166). Thousand Oaks, CA: Sage.

Coontz, S. (1997). *The way we really are: Coming to terms with America's changing families.* New York: Basic Books.

Franklin, J. H. (1974). *From slavery to freedom: A history of Negro Americans.* New York: Knopf.

Gaines, Jr., S. O. (1997). *Culture, ethnicity, and personal relationship processes.* New York: Routledge.

Gergen, K. J. (1991). *The saturated self: Dilemmas of identity in contemporary life.* New York: Basic Books.

Gutman, H. G. (1976). *The Black family in slavery and freedom, 1750–1925.* New York: Vintage Books.

Hill, R. B. (1971). *The strengths of Black families.* New York: Emerson Hall.

Hill, R. B. (1998). Understanding Black family functioning: A holistic perspective. *Journal of Comparative Family Studies,* 29(1). Retrieved from: http://firstsearch.oclc.org:80.webz/F

hooks, b. (1994). *Teaching to transgress: Education as the practice of freedom.* New York: Routledge.

Johnson, C. L. (1999). Fictive kin among oldest old African Americans in the San Francisco Bay Area. *Journal of Gerontology,* 54(6). Retrieved from: http://firstsearch.oclc.org:80.webz/F

Lewis, J. A. (1993). Farewell to motherhood and apple pie: Families in the postmodern era. *The Family Counseling Journal: Counseling and Therapy for Couples and Families,* 1(4), 337–338.

Mosley-Howard, G. S., & Evans, C. B. (2000). Relationships and contemporary experiences of the African American family: An ethnographic case study. *Journal of Black Studies,* 30(3). Retrieved from: http://firstsearch.oclc.org:80.webz/F

Schwartz, M. A., & Scott, B. M. (1994). *Marriages and families: Diversity and change.* Englewood Cliffs, NJ: Prentice Hall.

Taylor, J. T., Tucker, J. S., Chatters, L. M., & Jayakody, R. (1997). Recent demographic trends in African American family structure. In R. J. Taylor, J. S. Jackson, & L. M. Chatters (Eds.), *Family life in Black America,* (pp. 14–62). Thousand Oaks, CA: Sage.

U.S. Census Bureau. (2000). The Black population in the United States, March 1999. *Current Population Reports* (Series P20–530). Washington, DC: U.S. Government Printing Office.

Walby, S. (1992). Post-post-modernism? Theorizing social complexity. In M. Barrett & A. Phillips (Eds.), *Destabilizing theory: Contemporary feminist debates*, (pp. 31–52). Stanford, CA: Stanford University Press.

West, C. (1997). *Restoring hope: Conversations on the future of Black America*. Boston: Beacon Press.

White, L., & Rogers, S. J. (2000). Economic circumstances and family outcomes: A review of the 1990s. *Journal of Marriage and the Family*, 62(4), 1035–1051. Retrieved from: http://firstsearch.oclc.org:80.webz/F

Wilson, W. J. (1980). *The declining significance of race: Blacks and changing American institutions*. Chicago: University of Chicago Press.

■ ■ ■

2

The Peripheral African American Father: Is There a Black Man in the House?

Sylvester Huston, MA,
Terry D. Lipford, MA, and
Jeffrey Smith, PhD

Much of what is contained in the social science literature regarding African American fathers is pejorative in nature. African American fathers have been portrayed as absent from their families and uninvolved in the socialization of their children (McAdoo, 1993). However, although some African American fathers play minimal roles in the lives of their children, there are many who are daily, active participants in the lives of their wives and children.

The emphasis of this chapter is that African American men, as fathers, are present in the home, function effectively in their varied familial roles, and, most importantly, care for their children and families. The chapter first examines historical and contemporary perspectives of African American fathers and their roles and functions and then discusses implications for counseling professionals. The chapter concludes with an African American father's narrative of his experiences in raising two sons.

Historical Analysis

Historians have recently begun to emphasize the resiliency of the Black slave family and the complexity and strength of strong family ties that continued to exist even within the confines of enslavement. Perhaps one of the strongest ideas to surface recently has been the difficulty experienced by African American men during slavery. Family separation was a constant threat, and in reality, families were more often than not separated by the tyranny of slavery. Contrary to popular thought, marriages were remarkably stable, with most children born to slave families having the same father. The great majority of slave families were headed by two parents. As Wade (1994) asserted, it was not until the late 1960s, when the cumulative effects of poverty, racial discrimination, and segregation peaked, that the country's economic progress began to deteriorate, and the economy began to shift away from unskilled labor. A decline in the two-parent structure of African American families came into being during times of economic instability as racism and segregation rose to highest levels (Conner, 1988).

Although the power that Black fathers experienced was tightly circumscribed by the White slave masters, Black fathers continued to play a vital role in Black family life and provide resources that helped the family endure the oppression of slavery. During slavery, the majority of African American men overcame many obstacles and provided positive role models for their wives and children (Genovese, 1976). In many instances family gave meaning to the lives of Black men, and provided a method of coping with the brutal and exploitative nature of the enslavement process. As Gutman (1976), Blassingame (1979), and Genovese (1976) have asserted, perhaps the most salient outcome of the enslavement process— the chaining of Black men, transplantation to this country, and then the selling of those men as property—was the severing of relationships among family members.

The Great Migration to the North around the beginning of the 20th century brought about changes dramatically impacting fathers' position and role in Black families. The industrialization and urbanization that characterized the Great Migration period gave African American men opportunities for employment not often granted in the South. However, while many African American men pursued jobs in the North, their families remained in the South until the men earned enough money for the families to join them. This family separation, which could last up to a year or more, may have been the source of the notion that "there are no Black men in Black homes."

Nonetheless, many fathers remained attached and continued faithfully as fathers and husbands. Historically, many Black men in Africa and here in America understood their role(s) as father and functioned accordingly despite outside forces that impacted consistent ability to provide for their families.

Research on African American Fathers

The view of African American fathers and the relationships within the African American family have been shaped in a large part by the type of research conducted. Cochran (1997) noted in his review of the literature on African American fathers that prior to the 1980s, the literature related to the parenting role of the father was distorted, ignored, and largely minimized. Dominant societal stereotypes and the academic literature have served to provide consistently negative images of African American men as fathers (Mirande, 1991). Despite research that documents the role of African American men in all socioeconomic classes, the social science literature continues to concentrate on African American men at the lowest economic level. Research conducted on African American men and fathers at the lower end of the socioeconomic spectrum is often inappropriately generalized to African American fathers of other socioeconomic classes (McAdoo, 1993).

From a sociopolitical perspective it is perhaps helpful to keep in mind that early studies comparing abilities across racial groups were more often than not fraught with methodological difficulties that could call the results of those studies into question. However, most serious and sociologically important, not only were those studies published, but they were also uncritically and favorably reviewed. As Wade (1994) has suggested, the easy acceptance of these studies as representative of African American male psychology serves to support the stereotypes and myths cultivated by a society deeply rooted in racism and sexism.

Given that the vast majority of our social scientists are White males from middle- and upper-middle-class backgrounds, the role of the university and the type of research conducted is not surprising. The field of academic psychology has been described as strongly supportive of upper class bigotry. The suggestion has been posited that bigotry is so deeply embedded within the profession that it often subtly guides much of what its practitioners choose to investigate and interpret. Quintana & Bernal (1995) stated that over the past decade only 4.10% of the articles appearing in *The Clinical*

Psychology Review and *The Clinical Psychologist* were devoted to ethnic or racial issues.

Although the approach has been slow, recently the literature has begun to provide a portrayal of African American fathers that is much more accurate and representative. Cochran (1997) asserted that the inclusion of middle-class African American men in studies has contributed to a new direction in the literature (Ahmeduzzman & Roopnarine, 1992; Bowman, 1993). As noted by Staples and Johnson (1993), the frame of reference for early studies of African American fathers tended to rely almost exclusively on White, middle-class, western, mainstream families. The dominant theme in those early studies was invisibility—of a father either absent from the home or marginally involved in the day-to-day activities of an unstable and ineffective family unit (Bryan & Ajo, 1992). Contrary to these previous studies, the current literature portrays African American fathers like other men, as playing important roles in the lives of their families and children (Bryan & Ajo, 1992; McAdoo, 1993; Wade, 1994).

African American fathers may be viewed within the sociohistorical context of western patriarchy as being influenced by social norms that traditionally define masculine worth in terms of economic authority and power. However, economic power and authority have historically not been as available to the African American male. Limited ability to achieve economic power, authority, and self-sufficiency may serve to tightly circumscribe the role of the African American male within the family context. Economic vulnerability may result in internalized beliefs that undermine self-worth and lower self-esteem. Alterations in self-esteem and self-worth may predispose African American men to self-destructive behavior and a withdrawal from the family. Perhaps most striking are empirical studies that highlight the relationship between economic stability and fatherhood. Madhubuti (1990) argued that fatherhood can increase a man's sense of failure and vulnerability if he knows or fears that he cannot provide for his wife and children.

A study conducted by Liebow (1967) suggested that the inability to provide for one's family is a great source of stress and contributes to a marginal status within the family unit. The inability of African American males to be perceived by their White male counterparts as equals has had a direct impact on their ability to obtain employment. In a review of the literature conducted by Shinn (1978), socioeconomic status consistently appeared as one of the most important moderating variables in the relationships of African American men and their children. McAdoo (1986) noted a direct relationship between economic status and African American fathers' active participation in the socialization of their children. In general, middle-income African American fathers consider themselves effective and active participants in the upbringing of their children (Harrison, 1981).

Currently new research is dispelling the myth that African American men are absent from, or peripheral to, the lives of their children. Researchers at the University of Chicago, for example, have found that fathers involved with their babies at birth often continue to be involved with their children. Another example is an investigation conducted at a Baltimore prenatal clinic of 135 young African American mothers, fathers, and their preschool-age children. The average age of the children was 3, the average age of the mothers was 18. Among the fathers the average age was 20. Of the total men participating in the study, approximately two-thirds had completed high school and were employed.

Data from the Baltimore study suggested that 50% of fathers help in the care of their children. Researchers also found a direct correlation between earlier and later involvement. Of those fathers studied, the 75% who were the child's primary caretaker at birth continued to maintain that role when the child was 3 years old. Results also supported the notion that the father's levels of education and employment were predictors of the father's continued involvement with his children.

Implications for Counselors

Effective counseling and psychotherapy with African American men require that counselors have a firm understanding of the sociohistorical forces that have shaped and guided the role of African American men as providers and fathers. Racism, for example, has had a profound effect on the lives of African American men and thus the African American family as well. Practitioners can help African American men to view their situation within its sociohistorical context, to connect with their heritage and with the struggles of their fathers and grandfathers, and thus to develop realistic self-appraisal and a positive sense of identity. However, unless family counselors have a firm understanding of the developmental history of the African American male, the therapeutic journey will be perilous and fraught with pitfalls, myths, and misunderstandings.

When members of the counseling profession see the heterogeneity of African American men, and believe and understand that

Black fathers care and are present, equitable collaboration, rather than coalition between the powerful and powerless, can occur. Veiled strengths should become more apparent, and Black fathers can be seen and publicly treated as valued members of their respective communities.

Conclusion: Raising African American Boys— The Voice of a Father

Because the voice of African American fathers is almost nonexistent in counseling literature, this chapter concludes with a narrative from an African American father summarizing his experiences in raising two African American males:

> The births of my three children have been the most special times of my life. I have been blessed with two boys and a girl. My daughter is a beautiful African American girl with a healthy knowledge of who she is and her purpose. For this section, I will discuss my boys and my relationship with them. On October 16, 1979, and March 2, 1982, I watched in amazement as my two boys entered the world. I shed tears of joy on both of those days as these two strong, mighty, brown-skinned boys began to cry and see new surroundings. I also began to think about the awesome responsibility that I now had. I thought about my father and the respect I have for him. I remembered how he raised and provided for our family of six boys and three girls. I remembered the values of honesty, self-respect, honor, and family that he instilled in all of us. I smiled when I remembered the times I would sit in his lap and watch television, wait for him to come home and go grocery shopping with him, and the rides to church. As I looked at my boys, I saw my father and I understood now my role as a father. When we brought the boys home from the hospital, I did something that has become a tradition in my family since the viewing of a television program entitled Roots. One night as infants, I took them out in the backyard, raised them to the sky, and told to them these words: "Behold the only thing greater than yourself." I have lived and stressed this in their lives every since that day.
>
> As an African American father raising African American boys, I have found two things to be of utmost importance: roots and wings.
>
> When I refer to roots, I believe that you must anchor your children in the family unit, your heritage, and traditions. Also you must develop in them a strong cultural identity that involves your "things" or cultural objects, customs, and values. I began to anchor my boys at birth. I began to communicate to them daily by reading them sto-

ries, speaking to them in complete sentences, touching and hugging them, and telling them that they were special and the best. I sang songs to them, played music for them, read the Bible and poetry to them. The early years are the most formative for children, and I concentrated heavily during these years to help their roots grow deep. Time spent with my boys was very important. I made myself available for them and their needs. As they grew, I played their games with them. You could find me wrestling on the floor, playing basketball and football with them. We read stories together, did homework together, prayed together, attended church together, and ate dinner together. I was building my family unit, our heritage, and traditions daily.

My boys were taught that family is number one. We stressed that nothing would separate us. My boys were taught about themselves as African Americans. Just as the Jewish families teach their children about the Holocaust, I taught my boys about slavery and how we should never forget our roots, but learn and grow from them. I taught them about great African American leaders and their contributions to our world, and I taught them about the great kings of Egypt. Their early lives were spent developing the family unit, our heritage, and many of our traditions.

Teaching the boys was done not only with words but with my lifestyle. I taught my boys how to respect and love women by my actions toward my wife, their mother. I demonstrated respect, love, and concern for her in my actions, attitude, and mannerisms. They saw me honor and treat her as a queen. (While I am describing my role as father, the training and guidance of my children has been a joint effort of my wife and me.) My boys also watched as I placed my own mother in high esteem. My actions were just as powerful as my words.

Developing their cultural identity involved the "things" we had, e.g., clothing, games, art, food, our customs, holidays, family roles, celebrations, and our values or beliefs. Our "things" or cultural objects involved exposure to African and African American artwork, clothing of African people, and the eating of traditional African American foods. We celebrated the customs of our heritage, learned about Kwanzaa, honored the birthday of Dr. Martin Luther King, Jr., and learned about the customs of other people.

Values have been the most important aspect of the development of my boys. Their spiritual development was of utmost importance to me. I took them to church with me, prayed together with them, discussed themes of honesty and integrity with them, and demonstrated my love for God in my actions and words. I stressed that their love for God first and obedience to Him would guide all the rest of their decisions. The standard of excellence in achievement was a norm in our house. *The boys were expected to achieve.*

Nothing less than their best would be accepted. I also taught them about the world around them, the discrimination and biases that they would face, and their responsibility to love and give respect to everyone. I also taught them not to be naive but watchful, deliberate, and wise in their actions. Knowledge and respect of family, heritage, traditions, and a strong cultural identity are the framework for strong roots.

Wings are important in raising African American males. I provided the first wings for my boys. These were wings of protection. I provided protection by being the figure of strength in my family. I believe that the African American father must be the protector of his family. I feel that God requires, and my ancestors recognize, that I am ultimately responsible for my family. Together with my wife we raise the children and make decisions; however, the father must assume the leadership of the family and lead in humility and love. I protected my boys from the discrimination and bias of our society by speaking for them, supporting them in school, and not allowing anyone to speak negatively about them without being challenged. My wings protected them until I felt that they were ready to fly. They then developed their wings and began to fly as they grew and began to explore the world, meet and accept new people, and expand their horizons.

My boys are now fine African American young men who are quality individuals with a sense of purpose. One is in his second year of college, a fine athlete, and a scholar who received numerous academic awards in high school; and the other is in his first year of college, also a fine athlete, successful scholar, and creative musical genius. Each boy has deep roots in our family. They love each other, their mother, sister, and their father. Rooted in each is a strong sense of who they are, love for God, respect for elders, responsibilities to themselves and the world, and drives to be successful, prosperous, and meaningful men. They have been in public and private schools, yet they have never forgotten their heritage because they were rooted early in values, they were surrounded by love and high expectations, and as a result they have developed within themselves the internal motivation to be successful.

References

Ahmeduzzman, M., & Roopnarine, J. L. (1992). Sociodemographic factors, functioning style, social support, and fathers' involvement with preschoolers in African American families. *Journal of Marriage and the Family, 54*, 699–707.

Blassingame, J. W. (1979). *The slave community: Plantation life in the antebellum South.* New York: Oxford University Press.

Bowman, P. (1993). The impact of economic marginality among African American husbands and fathers. In H. P. McAdoo (Ed.), *Family ethnicity: Strength in diversity* (pp. 120–137). Newbury Park, CA: Sage.

Bryan, D., & Ajo, A. (1992). The role perception of African American fathers. *Social Work Research and Abstracts, 28*(3), 17–21.

Cochran, D. L. (1997). African American fathers: A decade review of the literature. *Families in Society: The Journal of Contemporary Human Services, 78*(4), 340–350.

Conner, M. E. (1988). Teenage fatherhood: Issues confronting young Black males. In J. T. Gibbs (Ed.), *Young, Black, and male in America: An endangered species* (pp. 188–218). New York: Auburn House.

Genovese, E. D. (1976). *Roll, Jordan, roll: The world the slaves made.* New York: Vintage Books.

Gutman, H. G. (1976). *The Black family in slavery and freedom, 1750–1925.* New York: Pantheon Books.

Harrison, A. (1981). Attitudes towards procreation among Black adults. In H. P. McAdoo (Ed.), *Black families* (pp. 199–208). Beverly Hills, CA: Sage.

Liebow, E. (1967). *Tally's corner.* Boston: Little, Brown.

McAdoo, J. L. (1986). Black fathers' relationships with their preschool children and the children's ethnic identity. In R. A. Lewis & R. E. Salt (Eds.), *Men in families* (pp. 169–180). Newbury Park, CA: Sage.

McAdoo, J. L. (1993). The roles of African American fathers: An ecological perspective. *Families in Society: The Journal of Contemporary Human Services, 74,* 28–35.

Madhubuti, R. (1990). *Black men: Obsolete, single, dangerous?* Chicago: Third World Press.

Mirande, A. (1991). Ethnicity and fatherhood. In F. Bozett & S. Hanson (Eds.), *Fatherhood and families in cultural context* (pp. 54–82). New York: Springer.

Quintana, S. M., & Bernal, M. E. (1995). Ethnic minority training in counseling psychology: Comparisons with clinical psychology and proposed standards. *The Counseling Psychologist, 23*(1), 102–121.

Shinn, M. (1978). Father absence and children's cognitive development. *Psychological Bulletin, 85,* 234–295.

Staples, R., & Johnson, L. B. (1993). *Black families at the crossroads: Challenges and prospects.* San Francisco: Jossey-Bass.

Wade, J. C. (1994). African American fathers and sons: Social, historical, and psychological considerations. *Families in Society: The Journal of Contemporary Human Services, 75*(9), 561–570.

■ ■ ■

PARENTING
CONCERNS

3

Parenting:
A Community Responsibility

Carla Bradley, PhD

The child-rearing styles of African American parents have been closely scrutinized over many years. These styles have often been mistaken as severe, possibly due to a lack of understanding and conceptualization of what is culturally functional (Denby & Alford, 1996). For example, national child welfare reports have revealed that African American children were overrepresented in neglect and physical abuse cases (Gelles & Harrop, 1989; Hampton, 1987; Tatara, 1991). On one hand, some child welfare researchers have associated these findings with the use of belt as a disciplinary tool within the African American community (Lassitier, 1987; Straus, 1991). On the other hand, a growing number of social scientists have suggested that the over representation of African Americans in the child welfare system may be a reflection of the inability of child welfare workers to distinguish between families that are "genuinely troubled" and those who are "well adjusted" but culturally different (Kelly, Sanchez-Hucles, & Walker, 1993; Peters, 1985). A study of child rearing of African American parents in the Midwest noted that African American parents only used physical discipline when their authority had been challenged by their elementary age children (Bradley, 1998). Peters (1976, 1985) also asserted that the strict, no-nonsense discipline of African American parents often characterized as "harsh" or "rigid" by mainstream oriented observers has been shown to be functional, appropriate discipline of caring parents.

Although the social science literature has begun to support the notion that there may be cultural differences in regards to disciplining children (Billingsley, 1969; Gray & Nybell, 1990; Hill, 1993; Saunders, Nelson, & Landsman, 1993), many African American parents are still being measured by westernized perspectives in child rearing. The problem may lie in the fact that many marriage and family counselors have imposed the view that strict and physical forms of discipline are violent and change worthy without giving credence to whether parents have the intelligence to properly apply firm discipline in the home. Although child welfare and social work literature readily acknowledge the need for cultural sensitivity in working with African American families, it is unclear as to what exactly this sensitivity entails and how it may be translated into policy and practice (Gray & Nybell, 1990).

To start, parenting programs could convey an understanding of the context of child rearing in African American communities and an attitude of respect for the values and concerns of African American parents. Historically, parenting programs and social agencies have encouraged African American parents to change their firm disciplinary techniques in order to incorporate the more psychologically oriented practices found to be effective in White middle-class families. These training programs may draw upon a somewhat alien model for African American parents. The problem lies in the fact these programs draw upon child discipline theories that primarily focus on democratic parenting styles. In contrast, recent studies (Bradley, 1998; Denby & Alford, 1996) have shown that African American parents place a premium on respect and adherence to authority from their children and impose severe sanctions when these rules are violated. Refining parenting programs so that they may also reflect the disciplinary priorities of African American parents might effectively assist African American families with parenting concerns.

The primary focus of this chapter is to lay the foundation for a culturally responsive parenting program. More specifically, this chapter examines the concept of child discipline and identifies themes and practices that meet the disciplinary goals and objectives of African American parents.

The Concept of Child Discipline

Most major parenting programs draw heavily from child discipline perspectives contained in the psychological and sociological literature. A survey of the literature indicates that prior to the 20th century, Protestant, White middle-class mothers were most influential in guiding the practice of child discipline in American homes (Hyman, McDowell, & Raines, 1978; Langdon & Stout, 1952; Miller & Swanson, 1958). Moreover, the ideas of child rearing were mainly given by White American middle- and upper-middle-class mothers who published their advice in books, magazines, and newspapers of that period. Most writers of that time advocated physical discipline and unquestioned obedience as well as love for the child. The doctrine of "parents know best" was generally accepted, and the superior vision by which this infallible knowledge was achieved went unchallenged (Langdon & Stout, 1952; Miller & Swanson, 1958).

The beginning of the 20th century marked a significant shift in the relations between parent and child. The concept of child-centered or child-oriented discipline permeated the consciousness of American society (Grunwald & McAbee, 1985). This new trend emerged primarily out of the social sciences in an effort to encourage parents to move toward a more democratic approach to discipline and allow children more freedom. Alfred Adler, a child psychiatrist who lived and worked in Vienna, Austria, was most influential in introducing this new approach to discipline to the field of family counseling. Adler believed that most problems that parents and children were having were a direct outgrowth of their poor relationships (Adler, 1930).

Dreikurs (1964, 1968), an ardent follower of Adler, extended and popularized Adler's ideas in the United States by applying his principles to the discourse of child misbehavior and discipline. Because Adlerian philosophy rests on the assumption of a democratic family atmosphere, Dreikurs challenged the arbitrary use of punishment (spanking, withdrawal of privileges) and rewards by parents as stimulants for behavior change in children. He believed the most effective means of discipline was the use of democratic, empowering methods such as natural and logical consequences that allowed children to experience the consequences of their own actions. From an Adlerian perspective, misbehaving children are discouraged children, so Dreikurs believed encouragement was also essential in improving and maintaining appropriate behavior in children (Dreikurs, 1964, 1968).

Another perspective that is closely associated with the Adlerian democratic model of discipline is the person-centered viewpoint. Based on the fundamental principles of person-centered therapy, Thomas Gordon, originator of parent effectiveness training (PET), developed an alternative method of discipline that involved children in the process of determining the rules they must follow (Gordon, 1970, 1988). Gordon (1970) believed children were more motivated to comply with rules or limits if they were given the opportunity to participate in determining what they should be. Like the Adlerians, Gordon also believed that the use of punishment and rewards was ineffective in stimulating behavioral change in children.

In direct contrast to person-centered and Adlerian perspectives are the ideas and principles of the behavioral viewpoint. The behavioral approach to child discipline, also known as behavioral modification, rests on the assumption that changes in behavior are brought about when that behavior is followed by a particular kind of consequence (Shelton & Levy, 1981). Moreover, Skinner (1976), the originator of behavior modification therapy, contended that behaviors that are reinforced tend to be repeated, and those that are discouraged tend to be extinguished.

Thus behaviorists recommended that parents use techniques such as "time-out" (removing a disruptive child for a short time from a situation in which reinforcers are present) and "response cost" (imposing penalties such as loss of privileges or fines for inappropriate behaviors) in conjunction with positive reinforcers to achieve desired behaviors in their children.

In summary, theoretical perspectives that dominate the child discipline literature appear to support a more democratic and child-oriented approach to discipline. Several experts (Adler, 1930; Dreikurs, 1968; Gordan, 1970) suggested that parents employ empowering methods such as encouragement and natural and logical consequences. Others (Shelton & Levy, 1981; Skinner, 1976) advocated more behavioral specific techniques such as praise, time-out, and withdrawal of privileges. A number of theorists (Adler, 1930; Dreikurs, 1968; Gordan, 1988; Skinner, 1976) either denounced the use of spanking or discouraged parents from using any form of physical punishment.

However, the literature also indicates that much of what has been written on child discipline has assumed a universal norm of parenting behavior. Moreover, several African American child care experts have asserted that the democratic approach to discipline is inappropriate for African American parents given the constraints that oppression has placed on the African American community (Comer & Poussaint, 1992; Harrison-Ross, 1973; Staples, 1976). For example, Comer and Poussaint (1992) contended that African American parents have the dual role of preparing African American children to succeed in an environment that is racist and often hostile toward African Americans. Consequently, African American youth are not afforded the luxury of give-and-take discussions with authority figures from the educational and criminal justice systems. Some African American scholars have acknowledged the appropriateness of using parent-oriented techniques such as physical punishment, obedience, and "glaring looks" (Harrison-Ross, 1973; Staples, 1976). Others advocated more lenient disciplinary measures reserving the use of physical punishment as a last resort. Whereas sketches of the child-oriented perspective are apparent in the African American parenting literature, the African American frame of reference appears to be antithetical to the mainstream approach to child discipline.

A Responsive Parenting Program for African American Parents

Because parent education programs derive heavily from mainstream child-rearing perspectives, most of the program topics and activities are geared toward the concerns of middle-class White American families. As a result, these programs may not provide opportunities for African American parents to discuss issues or concerns about raising African American children. A parenting program that presents diversified preventative messages and specialized parenting strategies might better serve the child-rearing needs of African American families.

Parenting programs facilitated by family counselors can provide an arena for African American mothers and fathers to process parenting concerns. The family counselors best equipped to respond to the racial and cultural needs of these clients in proactive and empowering ways are those who are aware of their own racial and cultural backgrounds and how their personal backgrounds impact the racial and cultural identities of their clients. A knowledge of the present and past experiences of African Americans is also important for effective facilitation. Family counselors must also be able to initiate open, thoughtful, and meaningful dialogue regarding the disciplinary priorities of African American parents. The following topics/themes can assist counselors with filtering through the child-rearing challenges confronting African American parents.

Topic 1: "What Concerns Me the Most Is..."

The disciplinary practices of African American parents have been highly critiqued by social scientists. A considerable number of comparative studies between White and African American parents have noted the prevailing use of physical punishment in African American homes. Consequently, when African American parents interface with human service workers they are often instructed that their disciplinary techniques are strict, antiquated, and change worthy. Little attention is given to identifying the parents' behavioral expectations or disciplinary concerns.

Recent studies (Bradley, 1998; Denby & Alford, 1996) have revealed, however, that African American parents are not preoccupied with the use of physical punishment. Moreover, these studies found that African American mothers and fathers overwhelmingly discuss problem behaviors with their children and only use physical discipline as a last resort with their preschool and elementary age children.

To this end, culturally responsive parent education training must begin by identifying how parents define discipline and what child behaviors are considered problematic. This can be done by showing parents a video of a child acting out. The facilitator can then ask group participants what would be appropriate behavior for the child and how they would handle the acting-out episode. This activity is most helpful in generating discussion among parents regarding their disciplinary goals and objectives and the results (consequences) of their efforts.

Topic 2: Preparing Your Child for a Racially Oppressive Environment

Another important issue that may impact the parenting behavior of African American parents is the role of racial socialization. As early as preschool, African American children are bombarded with negative messages about race (Tatum, 1997).

Denby and Alford (1996), in their study of African American parenting styles, identified four primary goals of discipline that were related to socializing African American children about race. These goals are to teach African American children (a) about situations they may encounter that relate to racial differences, (b) that they must work extra hard because discrimination against African Americans is prevalent in this society, (c) that life is not fair, especially for African Americans, and (d) that children must know survival techniques as they relate to race differentials.

To counteract the impact of these societal pressures on African American children, African American parents can use a variety of discipline strategies to prepare their children for an often antagonistic environment. For example, several African American scholars have acknowledged that firm, consistent, and sometimes uncompromising rule setting is needed to convey to African American children that although they live in a democratic society, they may not be afforded the opportunity to have democratic interactions with authority figures. For instance, recent news reports have revealed that the everyday practice of "driving while Black" can result in harassment and/or even death at the hands of the police. Moreover, a 2001 study conducted by the Oakland Police Department found that African Americans are 3.3 times more likely to be stopped and searched by the police than White Americans (American Civil Liberties Union, 2001).

Parents should also be encouraged to tell their children how they were disciplined and the ways in which they have negotiated racial challenges. This will allow African American children to link their family's past with present day experiences and obtain a greater understanding for their parent's disciplinary behaviors. It is also important for facilitators to expose parents to the life histories and racial encounters of other successful African Americans such as Malcolm X, Barbara Jordan, and Bill Cosby so that African American parents can incorporate these "proven" negotiation strategies in their child-rearing practices.

Topic 3 : Do Grandma's Disciplinary Techniques Still Work?

Social scientists have acknowledged that grandmothers play a significant role in the parenting of African American children. A small but important group of African American child-rearing studies examined the disciplinary behaviors of African American grandmothers and their role in the socialization of African American children. Hale-Benson (1986) contrasted the child-rearing techniques of 30 African American and White American grandmothers. The sample consisted of 15 African American grandmothers and 15 White American grandmothers who were between the ages of 55 and 85. With regard to child discipline, the study found that African American grandmothers placed the most emphasis upon disobedience, disrespect to elders, and talking back to adults. African American and White American grandmothers reported equally on spanking their children.

Pearson, Hunter, Ensminger, and Kellman (1990) affirmed that African American grandmothers were second in command (next to the mother) in the rearing of their grandchildren, especially if the family was a single-parent household. Their hypothesis was supported by a study they conducted on 138 African American families that included grandmothers in their household. The families were from a low-income community in Chicago. The study revealed that grandmothers were engaged in parenting behaviors such as control and punishment.

Wilson, Tolson, and Hinton (1990) had similar results from their study of 64 African American families with grandmothers who lived with them or resided next door. They also found that African American grandmothers shared the responsibility of disciplining their grandchildren.

However, Hill (1999) found in her study of 525 African American parents that mothers and grandmothers did not always agree on child-rearing issues, and conflicts often left mothers feeling that their authority was being undermined. Furthermore, several parents felt that they used less physical punishment and more communication than their own parents.

This intergenerational conflict is of particular significance to family counselors working with African American parents. Because kinship ties and extended family are of the utmost importance to African American families, it is crucial that family counselors create a supportive atmosphere for group participants to discuss these family concerns. The following discussion questions can be used to encourage African American parents to reflect on their present and future disciplinary behaviors and goals:

1. Describe the disciplinary techniques you have tried with your children. Which ones promoted behavioral change? Which ones did not?
2. How were you disciplined as a child? Are you currently using any of these methods with your own children? Which work? Which do not?
3. Were there any disciplinary methods your parents used that you thought were ineffective?
4. How would you like your child to function as an adult? What types of methods, resources, and experiences are you using

to prepare your child for adulthood? Which do you think are working? Which do not?

Topic 4: Parenting in the 21st Century

African American parents need to know that they are not alone in their child-rearing struggles. Life for African American children in this new millennium is more complex. They are bombarded with an abundance of information and have access to more resources. This stream of information may promote more questioning and challenging by African American children than in years past. As a result, African American parents today may not always have the comfort of saying, "This is what I say and that is it."

Family counselors working with groups of African American parents need to present current information on how other African American parents are navigating through the child-discipline challenges of today. Additionally, African American parents need to be exposed to the writings and thoughts of African American child-rearing scholars, clergy, and other significant figures in the African American community. Having such information and materials available to African American mothers and fathers will provide them with helpful tools for addressing their child-rearing concerns. For example, African American scholars such as Denby and Alford (1996) have suggested that African Americans parents rely on the following strengths of the African American family to direct their disciplinary practices:

It takes a village to raise a child. Parents can identify key people such as extended family members, neighbors, clergy, and church members to be "lookouts" for the safety and well-being of their children. These key figures can be instrumental in informing parents about their child's behavior and, at times, offer suggestions or support when parents are forced to take corrective action.

Oldest child as disciplinarian. Parents may identify times when the eldest child is given the responsibility of disciplining younger siblings. This is considered functional as long as the parental hierarchy is retained.

Parents can be supported in their choice to have older children assist in discipline of younger children, which should be guided and supervised by parents, maintain the hierarchal balance, and assure that the needs of the child disciplinarian are remembered (Denby & Alford, 1996, p. 94).

Other scholars have identified techniques such as withdrawal of privileges, discussions with children, and modeling as effective disciplinary methods with adolescent age children (Arnold, 1995; Bradley, 1998; Hill, 1999). Physical discipline has been deemed functional with preschool and elementary age children only when verbal warnings and discussion have failed (Barnes, 1985; Bradley, 1998).

Conclusion

Given the reality of increasing numbers of African American client families, parenting programs should have a comprehensive perspective of varied child-rearing practices in our society. Moreover, parenting curricula must offer African American parents effective ways in preparing African American children to succeed in a racist environment. Meaningful and constructive intervention requires family counselors to have a thorough understanding of the culture of African American parenting.

References

Adler, J. E. (1930). *Guiding the child.* New York: Greenberg Press.

American Civil Liberties Union. (2001). Is Jim Crow justice alive and well in America? *American Civil Liberties Union Freedom Network.* Retrieved from: http://www.aclu.org/news/2001/n051101a.html

Arnold, M. (1995). Exploding the myths: African American families at promise. In B. B. Swadnener & S. L. Lubeck (Eds.), *Children and families "at promise"* (pp. 143–162). Albany: State University of New York Press.

Barnes, A. S. (1985). *The Black middle-class family.* Bristol, IN: Wyndham Hall Press.

Billingsley, A. (1969). *Black families in White America.* Englewood Cliffs, NJ: Prentice Hall.

Bradley, C. (1998). Child rearing in African American families: A study of disciplinary methods used by African American parents. *Journal of Multicultural Counseling and Development, 26,* 273–281.

Comer, J. P., & Poussaint, A. F. (1992). *Raising Black children.* New York: Penguin.

Denby, R., & Alford, K. (1996). Understanding African American disciplinary styles: Suggestions for effective social work intervention. *Journal of Multicultural Social Work, 4,* 81–98.

Dreikurs, R. (1964). *Children: The challenge.* New York: Dutton.

Dreikurs, R. (1968). *Logical consequences.* New York: Van Rees Press.

Gelles, R. J., & Harrop, J. W. (1989). Is violence in Black families increasing? *Journal of Marriage and the Family, 51,* 451–470.

Gordan, T. (1970). *Parent effectiveness training.* New York: Wyden.

Gordan, T. (1988). Effectiveness training. *Person-centered approach, 3,* 59–85.

Gray, S. S., & Nybell L. M. (1990). Issues in African American family preservation. *Child Welfare League of America, 69,* 513–523.

Grunwald, B. B., & McAbee, H. V. (1985). *Guiding the family.* Muncie, IN: Accelerated Development.

Hale-Benson, J. E. (1986). *Black children: Their roots, culture, and learning styles.* Baltimore: Johns Hopkins University Press.

Hampton, R. L. (1987). Violence against Black children: Current knowledge and future research needs. In R. L. Hampton (Ed.), *Violence in the Black family: Correlates and consequences* (pp. 3–20). Lexington, MA: Lexington Books.

Harrison-Ross, P. (1973). *The Black child: A parents' guide.* New York: Peter H. Wyden.

Hill, R. (1993). *Research on the African American family: A holistic perspective.* Westport, CT: Auburn House.

Hill, S. (1999). African American children: *Socialization and development in families.* Thousand Oaks, CA: Sage.

Hyman, I. A., McDowell, E., & Raines, B. (1978). Corporal punishment and alternatives in the schools: An overview of theoretical and practical issues. *In Inequality in education* (pp. 5–20). Cambridge, MA: Center for Law and Education.

Kelly, M. L., Sanchez-Hucles, J., & Walker, R. R. (1993). Correlates of disciplinary practices in working to middle-class African American mothers. *Merrill-Palmer Quarterly, 39,* 252–264.

Langdon, G., & Stout, I. W. (1952). *Discipline of well-adjusted children.* New York: John Day.

Lassitier, R. J. (1987). Child rearing in Black families: Child-abusing discipline. In R. L. Hampton (Ed.), *Violence in the Black family: Correlates and consequences* (pp. 39–53). Lexington, MA: Lexington Books.

Miller, D. R., & Swanson, G. E. (1958). *The changing American parent.* New York: Wiley.

Pearson, J. L., Hunter, A. G., Ensminger, M. E., & Kellman, S. G. (1990). Black grandmothers in multigenerational households: Diversity in family structure and parenting involvement in the Woodlawn Community. *Child Development, 61,* 435–442.

Peters, M. F. (1976). *Nine Black families: A study of household management and child rearing in Black families with working mothers.* Unpublished doctoral dissertation, Harvard University, Cambridge, MA.

Peters, M. F. (1985). Racial socialization of young Black children. In H. McAdoo & J. McAdoo (Eds.), *Black children* (pp. 159–173). Beverly Hills, CA: Sage.

Shelton, J. L., & Levy, R. L. (1981). *Behavioral assignments and treatment compliance.* Champaign, IL: Research Press.

Saunders, E. J., Nelson, K., & Landsman, M. J. (1993). Racial inequality and child neglect: Findings in a metropolitan area. *Child Welfare, 22,* 341–353.

Skinner, B. F. (1976). *About behaviorism.* New York: Vintage Books.

Staples, R. (1976). *Introduction to Black sociology.* Chicago: Nelson-Hall.

Straus, M. A. (1991). Discipline and deviance: Physical punishment of children and violence an other crime in adulthood. *Social Problems, 38,* 133–153.

Tatara, T. (1991). Overview of child abuse and neglect. In J. E. Everett, S. S. Chipungu, & B. R. Leashore (Eds.), *Child welfare: An Africentric perspective* (pp. 187–119). Brunswick, NJ: Rutgers University Press.

Tatum, B. (1997). *Why are all the Black kids sitting together in the cafeteria? And other conversations about race.* New York: Basic Books.

Wilson, M., Tolson, T., & Hinton, J. (1990). The impact of two and three generational Black family structure on perceived family climate. *Child Development, 61,* 416–428.

■ ■ ■

4

Racial Socialization

Jo-Ann Lipford Sanders, PhD

I'm marked by the color of my skin. The bullets are discrete
and designed to kill slowly. They are aiming at my children.
These are facts. Let me show you my wounds: my stumbling
mind, my "excuse me" tongue, and this nagging preoccupation
with the feeling of not being good enough. These bullets bury
deeper than logic. Racism is not intellectual. I cannot reason
these scars away...every day I am deluged with reminders that
this is not my land, and this is my land.

—Lorna Dee Cervantes (1988)

Most children grow up within a family system whose members
bear primary responsibility for the socialization of the children. These early socialization experiences help children develop
culturally appropriate behaviors and find ways to meet social and
emotional needs (McAdoo, 2001; Powell & Yamamoto, 1997; Rivers
& Morrow, 1995).

African American parents have the difficult role of preparing their
children to succeed in a society that has a history of being hostile
and racist toward African American people. As early as preschool,
African American children are bombarded with negative messages

from authority figures about race (Owusu-Bempah, 2001; Tatum, 1997). Researchers have posited that the internalization of these messages by African American youth can lead to higher levels of anxiety and lowered self-esteem (Greene, 1992; Neal-Barnett & Smith, 1997; Phinney, Lochner, & Murphy, 1990).

A healthy sense of racial identity is needed to counteract the impact of these societal pressures on African American children. African American parents and socializers of African American children may employ a variety of strategies to expose their children to accurate and positive information about African American people and their history. This process is known as *racial socialization*.

This chapter explores the potential of racial socialization as a strategy for mediating factors of race consciousness in the construction of positive self-identification for African American children and offers insight into parental attitudes about the process. When working with African American families, counselors need to have an understanding of the socialization practices of the family so that they can develop and implement culturally relevant interventions.

The Mythological African American Family

The family provides the primary context for early human development and its influence significantly affects human behavior. Within the crucible of the family experience adults learn how to love and sacrifice, while children learn skills useful in understanding the world and their place in it. Lifelong relationships are established with family members that serve multiple purposes, including economic and social support. Within this milieu children are introduced to ideas that will impact the development of their self-concept and lead to traits and characteristics they will use to distinguish themselves from others. It is here that the very foundations of identity, worth, morality, spirituality, and value are laid. Although no absolute, objective definition of *family* exists, working models are often socially and culturally determined. The family, regardless of form, has been credited or discredited on the basis of the success or failure of its primary residents, the children.

The ability of the African American family to produce culturally healthy and socially productive children has been challenged by misguided inferences to a pathological family structure by researchers apparently unfamiliar with the true dynamics of the African American family (Hill, 1998b). For example, juxtaposed against middle-class White families, the African American family was historically described as disorganized, matriarchal, matrifocal, absent of fathers, economically disabled, illegitimate, and uneducated (Frazier, 1939; Moynihan, 1965; Rainwater & Yancy, 1967). "According to this formulation, family deterioration, both economical and structural, was the result of 'matriarchy' and its 'tangle of pathology'" (McAdoo, 1988, p. 7). The idea of inherent pathology has not withstood the test of time, reason, or research. For effective intervention, counselors working with African American families must look beyond mere structure to the functional dynamics. Rather than diagnosing failure to conform to a specific paradigm as causative in family problems, counselors must begin to seek optimization in the structures encountered (Burton & Jayakody, 2001).

Will the Real African American Family Please Stand Up?

The evolution of various forms and functions of African American families has been affected by a plethora of social factors. The family is more than just an incubator providing food and shelter for those inside. Increasingly it becomes clear that the family unit prepares members for survival outside of its domain. The construction of the African American family results from such influential factors as economic and social depression, race relations, ethnocentrism, and class distinctions. How families are constructed and function is obviously a factor of personally identified primary life issues faced. Therefore, in order to be effective when working with African American families, counselors should understand the context in which these families have evolved and are currently maintained.

> The unique African American family experience must be at the forefront of treatment; the influence of poverty, racism, a history of slavery, and continued dominance by the larger society must be considered. Finally, empowering Black families means assessing Black families within the context of their own unique experiences. (Williams & Wright, 1992, p. 35)

Hence, within the context of a race conscious society, the influence of race should be carefully considered when working with African American families (McAdoo, 2001; Owusu-Bempah, 2001).

Neatly organized labels and catch phrases cannot fully define or characterize the existing diversity of African American family structures. African American scholars have effectively disputed the myopic image of the African American family posited by early investigators. Through their efforts, several concepts tantamount to an understanding of these families emerged. These new concepts have successfully:

1. Dispelled the notion of a single African American family structure and given consideration to the diverse structures of African American families, such as extended family, fictive kin (those who are not blood related), kin helpers, and church family. Present day African American families are as diverse in structure and personality as were their African foreparents and are influenced by such forces as ethnic identification, self-identification, family composition, religious affiliation, geographical location, social standing, and economic status (Burton & Jayakody, 2001; Kane, 2000).

2. Highlighted the importance of understanding the *function* as well as the *structure* of African American families. Viewing these families from a sociological perspective has shown that functionality correlates with survival (Billingsley, 1968; Hill, 1998a; McAdoo, 1988).

3. Challenged the normalcy of a matriarchal model of African American families. The matriarchal model that typifies many African American families grew in response to a culture of slavery and its aftermath in which males were often forced to abandon the family for reasons of safety or economics. This form surfaced not as a natural evolutionary response but instead resulted from social and cultural stressors (Gutman, 1976).

4. Highlighted flawed research comparisons of lower class, poor Black families to the culturally defined traditional, nuclear, White middle-class families. These out-of-context comparisons rendered African American families as being not only different but also deficient (Hill, 1998b), and encouraged "research in which positive and negative outcomes are possible but not distorted by inappropriate paradigms, unsuitable methods, or transubstantiative errors" (Hayles, 1991, p. 379).

5. Encouraged the inclusion of African history, family patterns, and cultural traditions to provide a truer comparison reference for African American families.

6. Cited the influence of hegemony and Eurocentrism on factors affecting African American families, such as on educational, occupational, and economical opportunities as well as on housing (Williams & Wright, 1992).

7. Redirected research efforts and treatment interventions to emphasize the legacy of strength, stability, and resilience that belongs to African American families (Hill, 1972, 1998a; Howell, 1975; Mosley-Howard & Burgan Evans, 2000).

Whatever the structural makeup, there is consensus that African American families are functional, interactive, and capable of transmitting values, beliefs, and life experiences so as to lovingly produce physically and emotionally healthy children (Allen, 1978; Billingsley, 1968; Boyd-Franklin, 1989; Demo & Hughes, 1990; Greene, 1992; Hill, 1972; McAdoo, 1988; McAdoo & McAdoo, 1985; Peters, 1988; Spencer, 1983; Staples, 1974). Therefore, any investigation of developmental issues involving African American children should include an analysis of the resiliency approach used by African American families (Hill, 1998a; McAdoo, 2001; Stevenson & Renard, 1993).

The Political Hides the Social

"Times are a changin'!" Race relations have improved over the last three decades. African Americans can now vote and attend public schools; they no longer have to ride on the back of buses, drink from segregated fountains, or live in mandatory segregated neighborhoods. Overt threats from such hate groups as the Ku Klux Klan have abated. The presence of African Americans is obvious from the highest levels of government to the lowest echelons of academia. *Inclusion* is the buzz word of the day. In light of these changes, why should African American parents still feel a need to protect and prepare their children around the effects of perceived racism? Although a modified political climate may suggest an intolerance toward racism, endemic and engrained values posit its existence from a social perspective.

Until 30 years ago, the United States was legally segregated. Although legislated by law, discrimination practices were implemented and maintained by people. Because it is impossible to legislate morality, social remedies driven by laws attempt to legislate and direct behavior. Due to the pervasive nature of bigotry and prejudice, we often find these attitudes fully institutionalized, thus continuing oppression by default even as the individual consciousness of citizens is changing. Like participants in a masked ball, what often lies beneath the mask of social reform are the true agendas of those in power who seek to maintain the status quo.

The Tools of Life: Trainin' the Children

> Child rearing should be the primary concern of an oppressed
> people, and although the rearing of race men and women is
> obviously a stressful, complex and tedious process, it should
> be entered into at birth
>
> —Mari Evans (1994)

Socialization is a process parents use in child rearing. Older folks called it "trainin'." It occurs via modeling, through various forms of the media, through interactions with people (both within and without the family setting), through conditioning, and through direct and indirect verbalizations.

Guided by parents or primary caregivers, children learn societal roadmaps inclusive of customs, laws, symbols, cultures, and expectations. Children also learn such constructs as responsibility, authority, accountability, and power differentials. Power differentials in childhood are often attributed to sibling position or gender.

African American parents have a dual responsibility in child rearing. Like all parents, they have to teach their children to be proud of themselves, to function at varying levels of their development, and to understand their entitlement to high life goals. In addition, African American parents have to teach their children how to thrive and maximize themselves within a dominant monocultural social structure that often discriminates on the basis of skin color (Boyd-Franklin, 1989; McAdoo, 2001). They have to teach their children how to decipher rules established by institutions and systems—rules that are often unfair and based in social racism.

African American children do not have a choice; they must learn how to successfully interface two cultural experiences in such a way that they may define, develop, and embrace their authentic selves (Arnold, 1995). It is no easy task! As an adult, the late journalist Leanita McClain, writing for the *Chicago Tribune*, described this dilemma in her column, "The Middle-Class Black's Burden," in 1988:

> I run a gauntlet between two worlds, and I am cursed and blessed
> by both. I travel, observe, and take part in both; I can also be used by
> both. I am a rope in a tug of war. If I am a token in my downtown
> office, so am I at my cousin's tea…I have a foot in each world, but I
> cannot fool myself about either…Whites won't believe I remain cul-
> turally different; Blacks won't believe I remain culturally the same.
> (Cited in Coner-Edwards & Spurlock, 1995, p. 11)

One college student described the experience this way:

> Being a young Black male, assimilation is probably the most frequently used pattern of interaction in my life. In my neighborhood, especially with my circle of friends, it is a cardinal sin to assimilate with the White culture. We see ourselves as the shunned group. At every possible opportunity, we thumb our collective noses at White society. By learning the "rules of the game" a long time ago, I know that assimilation with the majority society is a must. When forced to assimilate, I just separate my two worlds. I'm always going to be Black with Black sentiments, and I'll never compromise that for anything. However, I will play by the rules dictated, at least to an extent, to further myself and my people. (Cited in Bucher, 1999, p. 11)

African American parents are challenged to provide this socialization without giving double-bind messages (e.g., "you are wonderful and able but you can't be successful in a world that doesn't want you"). They have to prepare their children for a race-conscious society and yet not psychologically immobilize the development of their children's authentic selves. Although the process is lifelong and life learned, most African American families successfully provide "trainin'" for their children to become biculturally competent.

Learning About Racial Attitudes

Racial attitudes are learned early through the transmission of values, beliefs, feelings, and perceptions about the effects of race, generally from significant others. Thus all socializers of children provide, implicitly or explicitly, socialization messages about race. However, ethnic and racial minority parents often place greater emphasis on the transmission of values, beliefs, and life experiences about race issues than do White parents (Benson-Hale, 1991). This emphasis is propelled by a need to prepare their children to survive, persevere, and adapt to lifestyles influenced by factors like class, gender, ethnicity, and race (Boyd-Franklin, 1989; Spencer & Markstrom-Adams, 1990).

Race consciousness is a two-edged sword that carries with it the potential for the emergence of prejudice, bigotry, and racial strife on the negative side and racial equality and empowerment on the positive side. In this country all too often we see this potential become reality as the negative consequences of racial oppression are played out in our daily lives. Many African American parents understand but are not consumed by the effects of racial oppression! Although they believe that race issues are not the only area of concern confronting themselves and their children, they also recognize the need for, and benefits of, directed intervention into this aspect of the socialization process. The result of positive socialization should be a healthy sense of oneself. The transmission of attitudes, beliefs, and values about the effects of race consciousness with the primary purpose of producing individuals with a healthy sense of self is known as racial socialization (Stevenson, 1994, 1995).

Racial Socialization

The term *racial socialization* has often been used interchangeably with the term *ethnic socialization* (Phinney & Rotheram, 1987). Although ethnic socialization may encompass racial socialization, racial socialization extends beyond an acquisition of behaviors, values, and attitudes about one's ethnic group (Greene, 1992). Stevenson (1995) defined racial socialization as the "process of communicating messages and behaviors to children to bolster their sense of identity given the possibility and reality that their life experiences may include racially hostile encounters" (p. 51).

Racial socialization, like all socialization, occurs automatically, at some level, simply due to active existence in society. However, socializers of children, residing in a context in which race has the ability to impact their lives, should organize the socialization process to purposively include proactive, protective (Stevenson, 1994, 1995), and corrective messages (Lipford-Sanders, 1996). A part of this process also involves the demystification and demythologization of cultural mores about Black people.

Racial socialization is also understood as a within-group psychological intervention—a mediating factor—to increase self-perception and a healthy identity in African American children (Greene, 1992; Powell-Hopson & Hopson, 1990; Stevenson, 1994). Mediating factors employed by African American parents include building the self-confidence and self-esteem of their children by becoming aware and proud of their heritage. This may be done through various modes of controlled media, by having them take part in culturally enriched activities, and by reading various histories and biographies about Black people (Bradley & Lipford-Sanders, 1999; Peters, 1976). The total process is one of education and definition.

Dimensions of Racial Socialization Messages

Stevenson (1995) explained that *proactive messages* focus on within-group identified strengths and accomplishments of Black people. Messages within this dimension include relationships between spiritual and religious beliefs, extended family caring, cultural pride reinforcement, and the development of coping strategies. African American children should be taught that within their unique cultural experiences and extended families there are strength strategies. These strategies manifest not only in response to oppression but also are a part of their legacy (Stevenson, Reed, & Bodison, 1996). *Protective messages* provide within-group or out-group focus. These messages expose the reality of racial discrimination and its potential to affect one's life. Protective messages encourage open discussions about race and are aimed to be specifically cautionary in nature. For instance, Black males might receive instructions about how to handle themselves if stopped by a police officer.

Lipford-Sanders (1996) pointed out that *corrective messages* need also to be included in the racial socialization process. These messages tend to be out-group focused. They seek to combat negative stereotypes associated with the worth of Black people. In her investigation of the effects of a fixed Eurocentric paradigm of beauty and its effects on preadolescent African American girls' perceptions and value of beauty, she reported that participants used the Eurocentric paradigm to assign beauty and worth to pictures of other African American females and themselves. Participants were aware of many negative evaluations of beauty historically assigned to Black women (e.g., skin color, hair texture, width of facial features). When African American girls attempt to define beauty, the process is believed to be threefold, they (a) redefine beauty including images similar to themselves; (b) assign a definition of worth and value; and (c) and accept a revised beauty paradigm. Positive, corrective racial socialization messages indicating the beauty and value of Black women effectively counter what Collins (1991) called a "Eurocentric masculinist aesthetic" (p. 88) that defined African American women as *other* and therefore ugly.

Researchers have documented that African American children whose parents provide positive protective, proactive, and corrective messages about the effects of race in a race-conscious society are better able to deter negative societal imagery (Sanders-Thompson, 1991), develop a healthy sense of self (Benson-Hale, 1991; Greene, 1990b), and are better prepared academically than African American children who have not received positive messages

(Bowman & Howard, 1985). Others reported that African American children who received little or no messages specifically about race were likely to internalize negative societal images about themselves (Greene, 1990a; Stevenson, 1994).

African American Parental Attitudes Toward Racial Socialization Messages

There is lack of consensus relative to the significance of racial socialization by African American parents (Greene, 1990b; Spencer & Markstrom-Adams, 1990; Stevenson, 1994). The significance of teaching African American children about possible societal attitudes regarding race is determined by such variables as age of parents, parental education, geographical venue of parent's family of origin, parental life experiences, the extent that the parents have internalized their personal racial experiences, and socioeconomic status (Boyd-Franklin, 1989; McAdoo, 1988). Although no one variable has been demonstrated to be more significant, parental influence is usually very strong; therefore, parental internalization of racial experience is most likely to be a decisive factor in the type of socialization children receive. Peters' study of African American parents reported that those who accepted and recognized the strength in their blackness made deliberate efforts to socialize their children "to cope with racial prejudice and discrimination" (1988, p. 43).

The first five parental attitudes in the following list are reflected in the literature. The sixth surfaced from various works in popular culture.

1. Protective parents. These parents feel that racial socialization is a central concern in raising their children. They provide messages about the Black experience in a race conscious society assuming a hostile environment. Children are taught to be proud and comfortable in their identification as Black people. Children who receive this type of purposive racial socialization also have a positive and knowledgeable sense of themselves (Tatum, 1997; Thornton, Chatters, Taylor, & Allen, 1990).

An illustration is the Hollywood actress, Halle Berry's recount of her self-identification as an African American woman. Halle, who is a child of a White mother and a Black father, says her mother told her that because of her skin color and facial features the world would look at her and interact with her as if she were African American. So her mother made certain that Halle was informed about the effects of race in the United States. Did racial socialization from a protective stance encourage Halle to deny her White mother or her White heritage? No; but her mother, seeing a biracial child with primary Negroid features and understanding how African Americans are affected in a race conscious society, chose to provide protective messages in anticipation of a society influenced by race.

2. Color blind parents or race transcendence parents. These parents aspire to raise a race-neutral child, one who does not see skin color. They believe information about race issues are the child's individual decision. These parents believe the goal of socialization is to provide culturally appropriate lifestyles, values, and morals, that is, to develop a good human being rather than a racial being (Sanders-Thompson, 1991; Spencer, 1983; Thornton et al; 1990).

Willie (1976), studying black families called to our attention a sentiment expressed by one parent about raising her son "without a color attitude believing he could decide at a later time in life his group identification" (p. 144). Ogbu (1983) stated that parents operating from this parental perspective are at risk, that they either have failed to understand the institutionalization of racism or have accepted the negative imagery provided by the larger society. Ogbu further cautioned that because of the lack of addressing racial issues in their personal lives, Black parents with this attitude are "ill equipped to instill a positive racial identity in their children" (p. 402).

3. "Make child bitter" parents. These parents do not talk about race at all believing that such discussions or information make children bitter, angry, and hostile. These parents fear instances when race or race issues are brought up. In addition, they believe that a discussion of race issues will render a child prejudiced. They further fear that an emphasis on race might "discourage children before they identify their potential" (Stevenson, 1994, p. 195). Often these parents are in denial about the impact of race or are repressing painful inculcation of their own life experiences affected by race.

4. "Only if asked" parents. These parents believe in the ideology of color blind parents and make child bitter parents. They prefer not to talk about issues addressing race. They provide information only when the child makes an inquiry. Then, only enough information is provided to answer the child's immediate question. These parents consider the construct of racism as too complicated for the child. They believe that an individual has to personally experience racism to fully understand it (Spencer, 1983; Stevenson, 1994; Thornton et al., 1990).

5. *"Things have gotten better" parents.* These parents believe that racial atrocities are events of the past and better left in the past. They cite many instances in which race relations are different now than when they were growing up. Spencer (1987) stated that these parents embrace a strong belief in societal institutions.

6. *"If you work hard" parents.* These parents believe race issues are something that happen to people who do not prepare themselves. In their quest for "preparation" they often push their children far beyond reasonable expectations academically and socially, for example, "nothing is affirmed except the grade of A." Although they never articulate it as such, they feel acceptance occurs if the symbols of success defined by the dominant culture are used as the frame of reference (e.g., individualism, competition, success defined as high economic status, and acquisition of status symbols such as cars, residing in the "right" neighborhood). These parents are easily embarrassed in the presence of Whites when their children are not on their best behavior, are critical of other Black parents without similar values, and often have an intolerance for inferences or conversations about race. They seldom side with their child against White authority figures and totally ignore or dismiss racial implications in any situation. They feel that African American children can work into societal acceptance. This parental attitude, which surfaces from popular culture, believes that through the acquisition of symbols associated with success, their Black children may buy themselves out of the experience of being Black. African American author James Baldwin (1995) described this attitude as parents who felt that "we had only to prove our worth and no one could deny our right to live in our country, as free as all other citizens" (p. 69).

Racial Themes

Thornton's (1997) study of Black parents' strategic use of racial socialization produced three guiding themes. He argued that racial socialization messages may be categorized by distinguishable domains identified as experiences:

- **Mainstream experiences.** Messages within this domain are race neutral. They reinforce the notion of equality of all, and emphasize the importance of achievement, hard work, and moral values.
- **Minority experience.** Messages within this domain are race referenced. They reinforce the restrictions inherent in racism

while teaching the relevance of being Black. These messages emphasize coping strategies in response to a race-conscious society.

- **Black cultural experience.** Messages within this domain are race centered. They reinforce Black heritage and Black pride. These messages emphasize Black historical struggles and successes, and might be considered socialization from an Africentric perspective.

Conclusion

Racial socialization is an intervention strategy used by socializers of children in a race-conscious society in the development of a healthy and positive sense of self for African American children.

Racial socialization is the responsibility of parents and others to prepare Black children to negotiate and advance in a society for which race matters. The racial socialization of Black children occurs simultaneously with battles against race-influenced privileges. It should not be allowed to inadvertently become a tool to maintain current attitudes. The effects of race consciousness represent very real stressors in the lives of many African American families. Counselors, educators, and mental health and medical health professionals may use this knowledge when working with African American families.

Several scholars have suggested that counselors can also incorporate racial socialization strategies into their work with African American children and adolescents (Boyd-Franklin, 1989; Bradley & Lipford-Sanders, 1999; Greene, 1990b, 1992; Lipford-Sanders, 1996; Peters, 1976, 1985; Stevenson, 1995). Utilizing culturally responsive interventions and providing African American children role models that can demonstrate how to handle discrimination experiences successfully are two avenues by which counselors can assist African American children in achieving a healthy self-concept. With knowledge of children and parental attitudes, counselors are in a better position to establish rapport, obtain accurate information, and formulate meaningful intervention strategies.

References

Allen, W. (1978). The search for applicable theories of Black family life. *Journal of Marriage and the Family, 40,* 117–129.

Arnold, M. S. (1995). Exploding the myths: African American families at promise. In B. B. Swadener & S. Lubeck (Eds.), *Children and families "at promise"* (pp. 143–162). Albany: State University of New York Press.

Baldwin, J. (1995). *The evidence of things not seen.* New York: Holt.

Benson-Hale, J. (1991). The transmission of cultural values to young African American children. *Young Children, 46*(6), 7–15.

Billingsley, A. (1968). *Black families in White America.* Englewood Cliffs, NJ: Prentice Hall.

Bowman, P., & Howard, C. (1985). Race-related socialization, motivation, and academic achievement: A study of Black youth in three-generation families. *Journal of the American Academy of Child Psychiatry, 24,* 134–141.

Boyd-Franklin, N. (1989). *Black families in therapy: A multisystems approach.* New York: Guilford Press.

Bradley, C., & Lipford-Sanders, J. (1999). Counseling culturally diverse young clients. In A. Vernon (Ed.), Counseling children and adolescents (2nd ed., pp. 195–214). Denver, CO: Love.

Bucher, R. D. (1999). *Diversity consciousness: Opening our minds to people, cultures, and opportunities.* Upper Saddle River, NJ: Prentice Hall.

Burton, L. M., & Jayakody, R. (2001). Rethinking family structure and single parenthood: Implications for future studies of African American families and children. In A. Thonrton (Ed.), *The well-being of children and families: Research and data needs* (pp. 127–153). Ann Arbor: University of Michigan Press.

Cervantes, L. D. (1988). Poem for the young White man who asked me how I, an intelligent, well-read person could believe in the war between the races. In Robhenberg, P. S. (Ed.), *Racism and sexism: An integrated study* (pp. 133–134). New York: St. Martin's Press.

Collins, P. H. (1991). *Black feminist thought: Knowledge consciousness and the politics of empowerment.* New York: Routledge.

Coner-Edwards, A. F., & J. Spurlock, J. S. (Eds.). (1995). *Black families in crisis: The middle class.* New York: Brunner/Mazel.

Demo, D. H., & Hughes, M. (1990). Socialization and racial identity among Black Americans. *Social Psychology Quarterly, 53*(4), 364–374.

Evans, M. (1994). The relationship of child-rearing practices to chaos and change in the African American family. In H. R. Madhubuti (Ed.), *Claim earth: Race, rage, rape, redemption. Blacks seeking a culture of enlightened empowerment* (p. 150). Chicago: Third World Press.

Frazier, E. F. (1939). *The Negro family in the United States.* Chicago: University of Chicago Press.

Greene, B. A (1990a). Sturdy bridges: The role of African American mothers in the socialization of African American children. *Women & Therapy, 10*(1/2), 205–225.

Greene, B. A. (1990b). What has gone before: The legacy of racism and sexism in the lives of Black mothers and daughters. *Women & Therapy, 9*(1/2), 207–230.

Greene, B. A. (1992). Racial socialization as a tool in psychotherapy with African American children. In L. A. Vargas & J. D. Koss-Chioino (Eds.), *Working with culture: Psychotherapeutic interventions with ethnic minority children and adolescents* (pp. 63–81). San Francisco: Jossey-Bass.

Gutman, H. (1976). *The black family in slavery and freedom, 1750–1925.* New York: Pantheon.

Hayles, V. R, Jr. (1991). African American strengths: A survey of empirical findings. In R. L. Jones (Ed.), *Black psychology* (3rd ed., pp. 379–400). Berkeley, CA: Cobb & Henry.

Hill, R. B. (1972). *The strength of Black families.* New York: Emerson Hall.

Hill, R. B. (1998a). Enhancing the resilience of African American families. *Journal of Human Behavior in the Social Environment. 1*(2–3), 49–61.

Hill, R. B. (1998b). Understanding Black family functioning: A holistic perspective. *Journal of Comparative Family Studies, 29*(1), 15–25.

Howell, M. C. (1975). *Helping ourselves: Families and the human network.* Boston: Beacon Press.

Kane, C. M. (2000). African American family dynamics as perceived by family members. *Journal of Black Studies, 30*(5), 691–702.

Lipford-Sanders, J. (1996). My face holds the history of my people and the feelings in my heart: The perceptions of adolescent African American females toward perceived facial attractiveness and racial socialization messages. *Dissertation Abstracts International.* (University Microfilms No 9716998).

McAdoo, H. P. (1988). *Black families.* Newbury Park, CA: Sage.

McAdoo, H. P. (2001). Parent and child relationships in African American families. In N. B. Webb (Ed.), *Culturally diverse parent-child and family relationships: A guide for social workers and other practitioners* (pp. 89–105). New York: Columbia University Press.

McAdoo, H. P., & McAdoo, J. L. (Eds.). (1985). *Black children: Social, educational, and parental environments.* Newbury Park, CA: Sage.

Mosley-Howard, G. S., & Burgan Evans, C. (2000). Relationships and contemporary experiences of the African American family: An ethnographic case study. *Journal of Black Studies, 30*(3), 428–452.

Moynihan, D. P. (1965). *The Negro family: The case for national action.* Washington, DC: U.S. Government Printing Office.

Neal-Barnett, A., & Smith, J. (1997). African Americans. In S. Friedman (Ed.), *Cultural issues in the treatment of anxiety* (pp. 154–174). New York: Guilford Press.

Ogbu, J. (1983). Socialization: A cultural ecological approach. In K. Borman (Ed.), *The social life of children in a changing society* (pp. 253–267). Hillsdale, NJ: Erlbaum.

Owusu-Bempah, K. (2001). Racism: An important factor in practice with ethnic minority children and families. In P. Foley, J. Roche, & S. Tucker (Eds.), *Children in society: Contemporary theory, policy, and practice* (pp. 42–51). Bristol, PA: Open University.

Peters, M. F. (1976). *Nine Black families: A study of household manage-ment and child rearing in Black families with working mothers.* Unpublished doctoral dissertation, Harvard University, Cambridge, MA.

Peters, M. F. (1985). Racial socialization of young Black children. In H. P. McAdoo & J. L. McAdoo (Eds.), *Black children: Social, educational, and parental environments* (pp. 159–173). Newbury Park, CA: Sage.

Peters, M. F. (1988). Parenting in Black families with young children: A historical perspective. In H. P. McAdoo (Ed.), *Black families* (2nd ed., pp. 228–241). Newbury Park, CA: Sage.

Phinney, J. S., Lochner, B. T., & Murphy, R. (1990). Ethnic identity devel-opment and psychological adjustment in adolescence. In A. R. Stiffman & L. E. Davis (Eds.), *Ethnic issues in adolescent mental health* (pp. 53–72). Newbury Park, CA: Sage.

Phinney, J. S., & Rotheram, M. J. (1987). *Children's ethnic socialization: Pluralism and development.* Newbury Park, CA: Sage.

Powell, G., & Yamamoto, J. (1997). *Transcultural child development: Psychological assessment and treatment.* New York: Wiley.

Powell-Hopson, D., & Hopson, D. S. (1990). *Different and wonderful: Raising Black children in a race-conscious society.* New York: Simon & Schuster.

Rainwater, L., & Yancy, W. L. (1967). *The Moynihan Report and the poli-tics of controversy.* Cambridge, MA: MIT Press.

Rivers, R. Y., & Morrow, C. A. (1995). Understanding and treating ethnic minority youth. In J. F. Aponte, R. Y. Rivers, & J. Wohl (Eds.), *Psycho-logical interventions and cultural diversity* (pp. 164–180). Needham Heights, MA: Allyn & Bacon.

Sanders-Thompson, V. L. (1991). Perceptions of race and race relations which affect African American identification. *Journal of Applied So-cial Psychology, 21*(18), 1502–1516.

Spencer, M. B. (1983). Children's cultural values and parental child rear-ing strategies. *Developmental Review, 3,* 351–370.

Spencer, M. B. (1987). Black children's ethnic identity formation: Risk and resilience of caste-like minorities. In J. S. Phinney and M. J. Rotheram (Eds.), *Children's ethnic socialization: Pluralism and development (pp. 103–116).* Beverly Hills, CA: Sage.

Spencer, M. B., & Markstrom-Adams, C. (1990). Identity processes among racial and ethnic minority children in America. *Child Development, 61,* 290–310.

Staples, R. (1974). The Black family in evolutionary perspective. *The Black Scholar, 5*(9), 2–9.

Stevenson, H. C. (1994). Racial socialization in African American fami-lies: The act of balancing intolerance and survival. *The Family Jour-nal: Counseling and Therapy for Couples and Families, 2*(3), 190–198.

Stevenson, H. C. (1995). Relationship of adolescent perceptions of racial socialization to racial identity. *Journal of Black Psychology, 21*(1), 49–70.

Stevenson, H. C., & Renard. G. (1993). Trusting ole' wise owls: Therapeutic use of cultural strengths in African American families. *Professional Psychology: Research and Practice, 24(*4), 433–442.

Stevenson, H. C., Reed, J., & Bodison, P. (1996). Kinship social support and adolescent racial socialization beliefs: Extending the self to family. *Journal of Black Psychology, 22*(4), 498–508.

Tatum, B. (1997). *Why are all the Black kids sitting together in the cafeteria? And other conversations about race.* New York: Basic Books.

Thornton, M. C. (1997). Strategies of racial socialization among Black parents: Mainstream, minority, and cultural messages. In R. J. Taylor, J. S. Jackson, & L. M. Chatters (Eds.), *Family life in Black America* (pp. 201–215). Thousand Oaks, CA: Sage.

Thornton, M. C., Chatters, L. M., Taylor, R. J., & Allen, W. R. (1990). Sociodemographic and environmental correlates of racial socialization by Black parents. *Child Development, 61,* 401–409.

Williams, S. E., & Wright, D. F. (1992). Empowerment: The strengths of Black families revisited. *Journal of Multicultural Social Work, 2*(4), 23–37.

Willie, C. V. (1976). *A new look at Black families.* New Bayside, NY: General Hall.

■ ■ ■

PART **III**

INDIGENOUS SOCIAL SUPPORTS

5

Africentric Rites of Passage: Nurturing the Next Generation*

Paul Hill, Jr., MA

One way to help African American youth become healthy, productive adults is to develop positive rites of passage that are based on their African heritage. These Africentric rites of passage provide youth with a strong connection to their past and give them the community involvement they need to move confidently into their future.

Adults are made, not born. The shaping of the adults we become begins early in life as the desires of our nurturers are subtly communicated to us in the ways we are held, what we are fed, how and when we are consoled, and why we are sung to or smiled at. This influence continues over the years as we are told what stories are worth our attention and what adventures are worth our energies. We are taught what to value and what to ignore. Eventually, we are ready to assume the rights and responsibilities of full cultural membership (Hill, 1992). Only then do we become adults.

In some cultures, the final entrance into adulthood is marked by a coming-of-age ceremony, a rite of passage into adulthood. Like other major life-change ceremonies that accompany birth, marriage, and death, the coming-of-age ceremony places the individual in a new position within the community. It is a critical moment of expansion, an entrance into a world of greater responsibilities, privileges, secrets, institutions, and understanding. It amounts to a second birth into a higher life of culture and spirit. The coming-of-age ceremony is an opportunity for the community to acknowledge this transition while renewing its myths and traditions and expressing its animating beliefs (Cohen, 1991).

Postindustrial cultures tend to view such ceremonies as primitive rituals that delude participants into accepting beliefs not otherwise found in the world of the intellect. Further eroding the validity of ceremony and ritual are the repeated disruptions and changes in society that have challenged nearly all of the comfortable assumptions that are, of necessity, part of any act of ritual acknowledgment. Because ceremony lives by continuity, not change, the coming-of-age rites of passage in their purest forms have disappeared from all but the most traditional and isolated societies. This is lamentable, especially when we recognize that the foundering of contemporary youth—their frantic searching for personal identity in intense, sometimes illicit experiences—is a symptom of the loss of a discernible threshold over which they can pass into adulthood. Without the ceremonial gateway to recognized adult status, the younger generation finds itself having to create its own coming-of-age rites of passage (Jones, 1984). The purpose of this chapter is to examine the basic principles of a rites of passage program and its benefits for African American youth.

A Modern Rite of Passage

Formal and institutionalized education is the nearest modern equivalent to ancient initiation rites that culminated in recognized adulthood. Both processes are compulsory. Both try to bend the unruly energies of youth to constructive social purposes. Both attempt to teach discipline and proper behavior. Both express and communicate the central values of the sponsoring culture. However, there are a number of significant differences between the old and new:

- Old rites were religious; new rites are usually secular.
- Old rites ran by sun and seasonal time; new rites operate by clock and calendar and are usually sedentary.
- Old rites focused on concrete experiences; new rites rely heavily on words, numbers, and abstractions.
- Old rites were dramatic, intense, and forceful, and had a definite beginning and end; new rites are slow, extended, and often vague about their ultimate destination.

- Old rites engendered awe; new rites commonly produce detachment and boredom.
- Old rites inspired participation in the ongoing history of the culture; new rites are often conducted in holding areas where youth are isolated from the larger cultural reality.
- Old rites resulted in an immediate and unmistakable status change; new rites provide no such direct deliverance into adult roles and status.
- Old rites were held at a determined time and witnessed by the community as a whole; new rites can continue indefinitely or end without any general community recognition.
- Old rites were conducted by caring adults who had the young participants' interests at heart; new rites are frequently administered by employees whose reason for participation is related to their own financial condition and interests.

Because schools do not fulfill the cognitive, physical, psychological, affective, and cultural requirements of a coming-of-age rite of passage, families and communities need to provide a process for transition from childhood to adulthood.

A New Problem, an Old Solution

The much-quoted and overused African proverb, "It takes a village to raise a child," is based on the assumption that healthy villages and communities exist. Unfortunately, healthy villages and communities are the exception in America. Here, we do not suffer from a youth problem; we suffer from an adult problem. Youth do not develop in a vacuum; they develop in unhealthy villages and communities that adults are responsible for allowing to exist (Some, 1993). This dilemma is not limited to the poor in the inner city, but is found among all classes, wherever they live. Youth internalize the values and emulate the behavior of adults. The unraveling of the wholeness of the individual and the degeneration of family and community life is a widespread problem. Nowhere is this problem more widespread and disproportionate than among African Americans.

The problem is recent. As oppressive as slavery was, African Americans were able to develop and sustain domestic and kin arrangements and create healthy communities. Prior to 1917, more than 90% of all Black children were born in wedlock. It has only been in the past four decades that significant changes have occurred in the African American family. Up until 1960, 80% of all

Black children lived with both parents. By 1990, less than 50% of African American children lived with both parents (Gutman, 1976; Staples, 1984).

An increasing number of African Americans strongly believe that the reinstitution of staging (rites of passage) within the growth process will give our children the springboard they sorely need as they prepare to take their rightful places in the adult community. In 1990, the governor of Ohio established the Governor's Commission on Socially Disadvantaged Black Males as a response to a growing crisis facing African American males in Ohio. Historical disenfranchisement, discrimination, inadequate education, and thwarted aspirations have often undermined the chances of African Americans to compete successfully and function productively in American society. The commission presented 112 recommendations for addressing this crisis in Ohio. The third recommendation was that the state "create, maintain, and sponsor rites of passage type programs throughout Ohio for African American men" (State of Ohio, 1990). There has been increased recognition of the need for positive rites of passage on the national level as well. The November-December 1995 edition of the *Futurist* forecasted "the use of Africentric rites of passage initiations as a solution for at risk young Black males" (Cornish, 1995, p. 6).

Looking to Our African Heritage for Guidance

The African ancestors of African Americans who were brought to America as unwilling immigrants had a tradition and history for adulthood development and regeneration of the community. These ancestors arrived as whole persons with a strong concept, cultural competence, high self-esteem, positive behavior, and group loyalty (Perkins, 1986). These African ancestors, through ritual and ceremony, always had a sense of their own destiny and knew whom they were, where they were from, and what their place was in society. Life was lived in stages that had special meaning and responsibility for each individual's life (Kenyatta, 1955; Turner, 1969).

Some of these African cultures held formal coming-of-age rituals. These rituals prepared their young people in matters of sexual life, marriage, procreation, and family/community responsibilities while fulfilling a great educational purpose (Ray, 1973; Read, 1968; Zahn, 1960). The occasion often marked the beginning of the participants acquiring knowledge that was not accessible to the uninitiated. Participants learned to live with one another. They learned to obey. They learned the secrets and mysteries of male-female relationships. African Americans have lost this rich African inheritance that is characterized by traditions of personal mastery and locus of control through ritualization of social relationships.

One of the devastating effects of the European slave system was that it caused much cultural confusion for the displaced Africans. New systems of thinking, acting, and working were forced upon the Africans as they entered the Caribbean and the Americas. Consequently, ritualistic and ceremonial practices that previously had great meaning for the Africans were suppressed or became so diffused by alien practices that their effectiveness in the lives of African people was diminished. The life of displaced Africans in the northern hemisphere has been almost devoid of this kind of staging. As a result, many African Americans are now characterized by a confused self-concept; cultural incompetence; ambivalent, adaptive, and reactionary behavior; depreciated character; and confused group loyalty. Negative inherited historical images and the market-inspired American way of life have sabotaged the efforts of many African Americans to achieve true manhood and womanhood (Akbar, 1987; West, 1993). By the time African American youth reach early adulthood, they may feel that much of the meaning has gone out of their lives. Because most of them grow up believing their options in life are limited, they begin to lose their youthful enthusiasm and optimism very early (Sims, 1976). Considering the problems faced by African American youth today, we need to seriously consider these African rituals and develop a modern Africentric coming-of-age rite of passage.

Africentric Rites of Passage

Historically, African rites of passage did not exist by any such name because African beliefs and behavioral practices were woven into the fabric of community life. It was not until Arnold van Gennep's *Les Rites de Passage* in 1909 that the phrase was introduced. Unlike his contemporaries, van Gennep felt that anthropological investigations should examine the rituals and ceremonies of African people and cultures to determine whether they had any inherent value for their practitioners. During his years of study, van Gennep identified the principles, beliefs, and practices that comprise the African paradigm for living. The African view of life revealed in van Gennep's studies is a journey through identifiable phases with predictable challenges or "crises" along the way. Each crisis is accompanied by specified rituals and ceremonies that facilitate an individual's movement along life's path. Rites of passage are the rituals and ceremonies that accompany a life crisis (van Gennep, 1909, 1960).

The African paradigm for living, which should serve as the basis for any serious discussion of rites of passage, includes the fundamental beliefs and principles that guided the individual, communal, and spiritual behaviors of the African people. Based on van Gennep's research, these may be summarized in part as follows:

- Humanity and nature are one.
- Both humanity and nature experience cyclical, periodic, and inevitable change.
- In nature these changes are celestial. In humanity they are called *life* crises.
- Both humanity and nature function by the law of regeneration, which states that the energy of all systems is eventually spent and must be renewed at intervals.
- In nature this process is symbolized as a death and rebirth sequence and is monitored by rites of passage.
- By definition, life crises are disruptive for both the individual and the community.
- The rites of passage that facilitate the individual's passage through a life crisis consist of three essential phases: separation (preliminal); transition (liminal); and incorporation (postliminal).

An African rite of passage based on the African life paradigm provided the framework within which an individual was guided through the psychosocial transformations necessary to successfully navigate life's cyclical, periodic, and inevitable changes. Moreover, it assured the community of a continuous flow of mature, confident, and socially conscious adults.

If we are to promote the development of African American youth into adults, we must use the African life paradigm to create new Africentric rites of passage. Africentric rites of passage provide a human development process that functions as a prelude to a metamorphosis to manhood, to adulthood, to wholeness. This achieved and recognized wholeness reflects self-knowledge, personal mastery, and an Africentric locus of control. Essential to the Africentric perspective is the understanding that the struggles of African Americans have historically had as their primary goal the gaining of some measure of human dignity in a society that too often disregards the culture of non-Western people. Africentricity promotes an appreciation for and use of the collective experiences of Black people in every part of their lives.

In addition to the African life paradigm and Africentricity, Africentric rites of passage should depend on a minimum moral values system—the *Nguzo nane* (or eight principles)—and rituals through ceremony. The eight principles are unity, self-determination, collective work and responsibility, cooperative economics, purpose, creativity, faith, and respect. These minimum moral values are important because they provide compass points for a community that help ensure consistent behavior among community members. The need for a minimum moral value system today is based on Maulana Karenga's Kawaida theory that "if the key crisis in Black life is cultural crisis, i.e., a crisis in views and values, then social organization or rather reorganization must start with a new value system" (Karenga, 1980). The *Nguzo nane* is the minimum value system African Americans need to develop healthy adults and regenerate their communities.

The Importance of Ritual

A ritual is the enactment of a myth, and myths are stories of our search through the ages for truth, meaning, and significance. We all need to tell our story and understand our story. What happens when a society no longer embraces a powerful mythology? To find out, read your local and national newspapers. The news is full of accounts of destructive and violent acts by young people. As adults, we have provided these youth with no rituals through which they can become members of the community (Campbell, 1988). When adults do not provide myths for youth through ritual, where do youth find their myths? They create their own. This is one of the significant reasons gangs exist. Why do gangs have their own initiations and their own morality (Perkins, 1987)? They have not been initiated into the community! Feeling the lack, they create their own community with its own rituals and value systems.

Ritual is the drama that brings meaning to the initiation process. Rituals should be used to begin a program (unity circle, invocation, and libation), mark transitions in the program, conduct the actual initiation ceremony, and bring closure to the initiation and formally disband the temporary community. When rituals are created for the rite of passage, elements of tradition as well as the creation of new traditions should be used. For instance, a rite of passage initiation ceremony might have the following general format:

- Processional
- Invocation and libation
- Statement of the Intention of the Ritual
- The opening council
- Chanting and song
- Drumming and dance
- Questions and charges
- The giving-away ceremony
- Grounding the participants
- The feast
- Closure (releasing the community).

Rituals were traditionally conducted by community elders, but the presence of the entire initiated community, or at least a representative of it, is important to show that the whole community is participating. Rituals through ceremony are important to internalize experiences. To become a rite or ritual, an activity need only be serious, established or prescribed by a legitimate authority, and formally performed at a designated time with symbolism. A ritual is a ceremony and can often be a celebration (Hare & Hare, 1985). Elements of celebration include honors that recognize personal and group victories, acknowledgment of new responsibilities, and intergenerational participation. In the celebration of the new initiates, the entire community acknowledges and honors its newest members for their achievements. The community may present gifts to the initiates as they are acknowledged and recognized as full and responsible members of the community. The ritual process includes a number of essential elements:

- Definite initial directions
- Emotional expression and promotion of the satisfaction of participants at each step in the process
- Consideration of other family members
- Permanent records (e.g., snapshots, journal)
- Appropriate recognition for the initial or culminating age period, age, year, or skill level
- Recognition of the process as an extension from the past
- Established future expectations of behavior
- Appropriate and accurate references to African customs through research.

Steps in the Right Direction

A number of well-entrenched groups in African American communities already have comprehensive life cycle rites of passage. These rites of passage provide a foundation for the groups to regulate and supervise their members. Often these groups establish life cycle rites to address the holistic developmental needs of the community. These rites may include education, youth programs, ongoing cultural events, celebration of African American holidays and ancestors, naming ceremonies, and weddings. Some of these groups have established regular acknowledgments of the rites by age group. Some have established guidelines for approximate changes in life cycle development. Still others suggest an acknowledgment by conducting a celebration every 7 years: at birth, the naming ceremony is performed; at approximately age 14, the puberty rite is performed; at age 28 a ceremony may mark the entry to adulthood; and at around age 63 eldership status and honor is recognized (Coppock, 1990).

Conclusion: Return and Fetch It

Rites of passage for the African American community must be Africentric and grounded in a minimum moral value system, such as the *Nguzo nane*. A thorough understanding and operation of such a process and its values are crucial. Rites of passage as a process of life cycle development and community regeneration were an essential part of African tradition that must be resurrected to develop youth and regenerate the community. Africentric rites of passage provide an excellent change model for developing positive values, attitudes, and behaviors among African American youth. Our ability to nurture a new generation of African American adults through Africentric rites of passage is limited only by the creativity of those wishing to reestablish the way. What has been presented is something old that has been rediscovered, something that has been returned to us through our African ancestors with the following invitation, "Return and fetch it."

Family counselors can enhance the well-being of African American youth by encouraging them to participate in this type of developmental training and incorporating the principles of rites of passage in their counseling practice. Ignoring the racial disparities that exist in the lives of African American children can be perceived as an insult to African American adolescents, in particular, who are often hit the hardest with negative race-based attitudes from the general public (Alford, McKenry & Gavazzi, in press). Adolescence is a critical time for African American youth. In addition to dealing with the normative, cognitive, physical, and social issues characteristic of adolescent children, African American adolescent males must also work through developmental issues specific to their race and gender. The rites of passage experience can help African American male youth process this additional and critical developmental step that has often been often overlooked.

References

Akbar, N. (1987). *Chains and images of psychological slavery.* Jersey City, NJ: New Mind Productions.

Alford, K. A., McKenry, P. C., & Gavazzi, S. M. (in press). Enhancing achievement in adolescent Black males: The rites of passage link. In R. Majors (Ed.), *Race and education in Britain.*

Campbell, J. (1988). *The power of myth.* New York: Doubleday.

Cohen, D. (1991). *The circle of life.* San Francisco: Harper.

Coppock, N. (1990). *Africentric theory and applications: Vol. 1. Adolescent rites of passage.* Washington, DC: Baobab.

Cornish, E. (1995, November-December). Outlook "96." *Futurist, 29*(6), 6.

Gutman, H. (1976). *The Black family in slavery and freedom, 1750–1925.* New York: Pantheon.

Hare, N., & Hare, J. (1985). *Bringing the Black boy to manhood: The passage.* San Francisco: Black Think Tank.

Hill, P. (1992). *Coming of age.* Chicago: African American Images.

Jones, T. (1984, Summer). Growing up modern. *Creative Living: The Magazine of Life, 13*(3), 2.

Karenga, M. (1980). *Kawaida theory.* Inglewood, CA: Kawaida.

Kenyatta, J. (1955). *Facing Mount Kenya.* New York: Vintage.

Perkins, U. (1986). *Harvesting new generations.* Chicago: Third World Press.

Perkins, U. (1987). *Explosion of Chicago's Black gangs.* Chicago: Third World Press.

Ray, B. (1973). *African religions: Symbols, ritual, and community.* Englewood Cliffs, NJ: Prentice Hall.

Read, M. (1968). *Children of their fathers: Growing up among the Ngoni of Malawi.* New York: Holt, Rinehart & Winston.

Sims, E., Jr. (1976). *Rites of passage program for Black youth.* Self-published with the assistance of the United Church Board for Homeland Ministries, New York. (Available from the Black Ecumenical Commission, Boston.)

Some, M. (1993). *Ritual*. Portland, OR: Swan Raven.

Staples, R. (1984). *Black masculinity*. San Francisco: Black Scholar Press.

State of Ohio. (1990). *Ohio's African American males: A call to action* (Report of the Governor's Commission on Socially Disadvantaged Black Males). Columbus: Ohio Office of Black Affairs.

Turner, V. (1969). *The ritual process*. Ithaca, NY: Cornell University Press.

van Gennep, A. (1909). *Les rites de passage* (M. B. Vizedem & G. B. Caffee, Trans.). Paris: Nourry.

van Gennep, A. (1960). *The rites of passage*. Chicago: University of Chicago Press.

West, C. (1993). *Race matters*. Boston: Beacon.

Zahn, D. (1960). *Société d' initiation* [Society of initiation]. Paris: Mouton.

■ ■ ■

6

The Black Church:
Bridge Over Troubled Water

Rufus G. W. Sanders, PhD

> Beyond its purely religious function, as critical as that func-
> tion has been, the Black church in its historical role as lyceum,
> conservatory, forum, social service center, political academy
> and financial institution has been and is for Black America the
> mother of our culture, the champion of our freedom, the hall-
> mark of our civilization.
>
> —C. Eric Lincoln (1990, p. 10)

One of the primary sources of support for many African American people is spirituality. This spirituality is often tied in with
some form of organized religion. The organized Black church is the
oldest and most influential institution founded, maintained, and
controlled by Black people. Investigators of African American families have acknowledged its significance and foundational importance
to the development and survival of African Americans in American
culture (Billingsley, 1992; Boyd-Franklin, 1989; Frazier, 1939; June,
1991; Locke; 1992). Even when African Americans "raised in the
church" (early socialization of values provided by church attendance)
as children become adults and cease regular church attendance,

moral values learned from this institution often frame their worldview (Brisbane & Womble, 1985–1986).

African American religion developed within the larger context of American democracy. It emerged initially under slavery and mercantile capitalism during the pre-Civil-War period. Although African American religion underwent some institutionalization at this time under the independent Black church movement, its development in the form of a wide array of organized sects and denominations occurred after the Civil War and was concurrent with the development of industrial capitalism in both the North and the South. People of African ancestry actually helped to shape American Christianity (as well as Judaism and Islam in some cases) into various forms to meet their own needs and to serve as the single social institution that, for many generations, they could call their own.

To a large extent, African American religion is a reworked Christianity. It has its own character, style, and outlook. It is a church that syncretized elements of African religion and Euro-Christianity as well as Islamic and Judaic sectarianism. The end result was a true American institution—the Black church.

According to Frazier (1964), African American religion has historically functioned as a "refuge in a hostile world" (p. 12). African Americans and their families have utilized their religion and spirituality as a way of creating space in addressing the vagaries of racism and class stratification.

This chapter discusses the Black church's influence on African American families; highlights its historical evolution and its social and strength agencies, and offers implications for counseling. The focus is on organized Christian bodies, although no particular denomination (such as Baptist, Methodist, or Pentecostal) is featured.

The Importance of the Black Church

Understanding the religion and spirituality of a people is key to understanding their culture. Religion and spirituality touch the very core of a people and therefore become a prism of true transparency. An examination of religion and spirituality provides priceless knowledge about the essentiality and foundational entities out of which came the particularities that make a culture unique and ethnocentric.

The cosmology of black Americans is related to both their African heritage and their conversion to Euro-Christianity. This is the syncretic aspect of African American culture. Black people have created their own form of culture using a cosmos that is parallel to, rather than a replication of, American culture. Therefore, contrary to former thought, the Black church, as a Black religious experience, is not a duplication of the White church in America. The Black American church, whatever the denomination, is actually a collage produced by syncretism, assimilation, and acculturation. It is a mixture of Africanism, emotionalism, legalism, ritualism, and theological intellectualism. Other Africans of the diaspora also used African deities as a base for their new syncretic religions once they arrived in the New World. Examples of these religions include the Voudou of Haiti, the Obeja of Jamaica, the Santeria of Cuba, and the Umbanda of Brazil. These African-based religions played a major role in the worship services and lives of the African people who had been transported against their will. These religions, now with Christianity also a part of their syncretic mix, remain a prominent part of the Haitian, Jamaican, Cuban, and Brazilian cultures.

To exclude the Black church from the study of the African American family is not only to greatly distort the history of the American Christian church but also to negate the impact that the Black church has had on all aspects of American as well as African American life. The church's role as a vanguard of the freedom movement, the gains that emerged from the church's freedom struggle, such as the Civil Rights Movement and affirmative action programs, benefited both Black America and White America.

Lincoln (1990) characterized the church as a dialectical institution. This model, based on the work of Nelsen and Kuserner-Nelsen (1975), sees the Black church as an institution involved in polar activities—social and prophetic. The tension between these poles shifts and changes in historical time, with the changes dependent on the cultural climate and social conditions at any given time.

According to DuBois (1903), the Black church represents the collective double consciousness of African Americans. Blacks are both African and American. The church is both a social institution and a religious body that moves along a dynamic continuum. As a social institution, the church becomes a complex cultural structure; as a religious body, it is just as complex.

Early studies of the Black church ignored its dialectic nature as well as the double consciousness of African Americans perceived by DuBois. Although the studies did recognize the church's multifaceted nature, they totally ignored the tension of its meaning. They looked at only one side of the polarity, and thus described a rather simple, backward, emotional, exotic, and strangely ambiguous institution. Many scholars have therefore seriously misunderstood the complex nature of the Black church.

Recently, however, Lincoln, in *The Black Church in the African American Experience* (1990) and Billingsley, in *Climbing Jacob's Ladder: The Enduring Legacy of the African American Family* (1992), have reassessed the importance of the Black church. Both of these post-1960s social intellectuals looked at the church in a holistic manner and emphasized that the Black church has played a complex role in and indeed has been the epicenter of the Black community. Both saw that the Black church is and has been the "bridge over troubled water" for African American families.

In their works, Lincoln and Billingsley wrote optimistically and reverently about the Black church. For example, Lincoln noted that "the Black church is the mother of our culture, the champion of our freedom, the hallmark of our civilization" (1990, p. 63). And Billingsley (1968) stated so clearly what the church is and what its mission has historically been:

> ...the Black church as an institution has always reached out to serve important functions for the Black community as a whole. It is in this respect both a preserver of the African American heritage and an agent for reform. Indeed no successful movement for improving the conditions of life for the African American people has been mounted without the support of the church. (p. 350)

Historical Overview of the Black Church

"Religion Threatened My Soul"

In studying any phase of the character and the development of the religious, social, family, and cultural life of Blacks in the United States, we must first recognize the manner in which Africans were captured, selected for enslavement, and stripped of their social and cultural heritage. The capture of most Africans was in intertribal wars; most of the Africans captured and enslaved were males. Those African males selected for the slave markets on the African coasts were the young and most vigorous (Frazier, 1964). Given that young men are generally agreed to be poor bearers of the cultural heritage of a people (Frazier, 1964), it is easy to get an idea of how this selective process both damaged the family structures and family roles of enslaved Africans and reduced to a minimum the possibility of retention and transmission of African culture. This selective process for males continued until approximately 1840 when the number of African females equaled the number of males in the slave population of the United States.

The barracoons—or concentration-camp-like barracks—in which the enslaved Africans were held until they were transported to the United States further stripped their social and cultural heritage. The captured Africans were confined within the barracoons without regard for gender, family ties, language, or tribal affiliation until cargo purchase for the slave market in the New World was requested. Then came the long voyage across the Atlantic Ocean—the Middle Passage—during which the enslaved Africans were packed, spoon fashion, into the slave ships.

The final steps in stripping the enslaved Africans of their social and cultural heritage came when they reached the New World. On the large sugar and cotton plantations in the Southern states, there was little contact between Whites and the enslaved Africans, and thus there were some opportunities for the enslaved Africans to reestablish cultural heritage. However, the majority of enslaved Africans were held in small groups on small farms and plantations (Frazier, 1964). Further, there were even fewer slaves per holding in some of the upland cotton regions of Alabama, Mississippi, Louisiana, and Arkansas (Rogers, 1971). Whatever the size of the farm or plantation, new imports had to be broken into its regime. According to descriptions given by a traveler in Louisiana, the newly enslaved Africans were made to bathe often and then distributed in small numbers among the old slaves in order to speed up acquisition of slave habits (Rogers, 1971). Noteworthy is that the captives were often purposely separated based on language and tribal affiliation in order to prevent escape attempts. Any effort by the enslaved Africans to preserve or use their native languages was prohibited. A general rule was that there could be no assembly of five or more of the captured without the presence of a White male. This applied especially to gatherings for religious purposes. All of these steps furthered the loss of cultural heritage (Lester, 1968). However, it is here that resiliency appears and skills for family survival materialize. Individuals unfamiliar with each other's language and customs nevertheless employed homogeneous African values, reinvented family structures, and buffered the atrocities of slavery.

Slavery differed from country to country, but in the United States the system that evolved has no comparisons in its far-reaching cruelty (Lester, 1968). No other country in which Africans were enslaved destroyed their cultural traditions to such an extent. Only fragments of African tradition remain in African American culture, whereas in South America and the Caribbean Islands, where slavery was also prevalent, African religions, music, language, and family patterns still exist today.

The enslavement of Africans not only destroyed the traditional African system of kinship and other forms of organized social life but also made insecure and precarious the most elementary form of social life—the family. There were no legal marriages for enslaved Africans. The relationships of the husband to his wife and the father to his children were dependent upon the will of the White masters (Lester, 1968). Under the most favorable conditions of slavery (e.g., among the privileged skilled artisans or favored house servants), some stability in family relations and a feeling of solidarity among the members of the slave household did develop. This represented the maximum permitted social cohesion (Gutman, 1976; Lester, 1968). Thus it was not what remained of African culture or African religious experiences but the adding of the Western Christian religious experience that provided the new basis of social cohesion among a people who had been stripped of their social and cultural heritage and who lacked a structured social life.

"Religion Made Me Whole"

The Black church became the main arena of social life in which demoralized individuals could achieve distinction and status. It was the area in which Blacks secretly struggled for freedom and in which their thirst for empowerment could be satisfied. It was especially important to Black males who had never been able to assert themselves and assume the dominant male role, especially in family relations, as defined by American culture. The Black church became a forum for political life for Black leaders. Although denied the right to be recognized as citizens and hence denied the right to vote, within their churches, they could vote and elect church officers. It also had political significance for Black people in a broader sense.

The development of the Black family was also tied largely to the development of the Black church. A study of Black churches in a Black-belt county in Georgia in 1903 revealed that a large proportion of the churches were "family churches." The church represented the only other organized social entity outside the family. Many rural Black communities in the South were named after their churches (Rogers, 1971). The Christian Bible influenced the governance of the Black church as well as of many Black families. As absolute power was sanctioned for the church, so was absolute power for the father in enslaved African families. The church became and remains the most important agency of social control among Blacks.

For example, the church could implement censure for unconventional and immoral sexual behavior and could punish those who violated monogamous mores by expulsion and excommunication.

Despite experiencing disparagement and domination by Whites, the Black church remained a refuge. What mattered for African Americans was the way they were treated in the church. What also mattered was that the church was truly a place for self-expression and status as well as a literal haven from the insanity of oppression, subjugation, discrimination, and social isolation.

The Church as a Social Agent

Critics of the power of the Black church say that the church no longer lives up to the expectations engendered by its past. They say that the Black church may be more important in the lives of women than men. They say that fragmentation and complacency have led to the church abandoning the Black underclass (Rogers, 1971). They also say that the religiosity, educational attainment of its leaders, and economic gains over the last decades have encouraged divisiveness, triviality, and consequent betrayal of both Christianity and Black people (Washington, 1964). Despite these criticisms, most still acknowledge the glorious accomplishments of the church historically. As Wardell Payne, director of the Institute for Black Religious Bodies at Howard University Divinity School, has appropriately summarized, "...the Black church is still the strongest institution we have in the Black community" (cited in Hawkins, 1993, p. 16).

The sociocultural significance of the Black church is undeniable. The Black church has always interacted within the spheres of politics, economics, education, and culture. The Black church has always negotiated and obtained things necessary for living (i.e., housing, jobs, health and child care, and clothing). Educational opportunities for Black people en masse are attributable to the efforts of the Black church. In the last years of the 20th century, the Black church reached even more deeply into the realms of social service, social change, and politics to nurture the spirit of its people and families. Its influence was perhaps most apparent during the Civil Rights Movement of the 1960s when church-based groups not only helped develop strategies and leaders but also sustained the movement.

Many Black churches, called "vital congregations" by Bishop Nichols, a retired bishop in the United Methodist Church (Billingsley, 1992), are "building senior citizens housing projects, schools, medical clinics, buying and rehabilitating housing and business strips, and funding new business ideas" (Madhubuti, 1994, p. 226). They are also involved in homeless shelters, feeding programs, nursing home programs, clinical counseling programs, fitness centers, prison ministries, rites of passage programs for adults and youths, and GED preparation programs. They have heeded the cry of the kings and queens of Africa and returned to the redemptive and liberating principles through which the real needs of Black people are met within the context of their personal and social situations (Billingsley, 1992; Locke, 1992). The Black church has a rich heritage for social involvement in its communities. It has and will probably always be the bridge over troubled waters.

The Church as a Strength Agent

The structure of the Black church and the roles of its leaders and members parallels those of the Black family and can serve as agents to strengthen, and to provide social support for, the Black family.

Church Structure as a Strength Agent

The congregation of the church serves as an extended family and is often referred to as *church family*. Congregation members are identified as *brother*, *sister*, or *mother*. These titles facilitate enduring attachments and suggest not only a kinship beyond blood ties but also a kinship in which members serve in similar roles as those identified within American culture.

Church Roles as Strength Agents

The minister, most often referred to as *pastor* or *elder*, and his wife are seen as the father and mother of the church family. Regardless of the age of the pastor, he or she may be regarded as father even by senior citizens within the church and Black communities. As father, the minister is also the family counselor and confidante. African American ministers have been recognized as major leaders in their communities. He or she is involved in multiple aspects of congregation members' family life and is often part of any major decision made by the family. To illustrate:

- A deacon at a local church was diagnosed with lung cancer. After his doctor's visit (before he called his wife) he went to see his pastor. After chemotherapy treatments (received in consultation with his pastor) he became very ill. During his stay in intensive care, a life or death decision about his care needed to be made. His wife told the doctor that she could not make this decision without consulting with her minister.

- A young man warring against the effects of schizophrenia stopped taking his medicine and began acting out. Although his mother hospitalized him for safety reasons, she refused to talk about extended care until her minister arrived.

Ministers may be extremely influential in and beneficial to the counseling process. Clients should be asked early in the counseling process about the significance of their minister or spiritual leader.

Church Parenting as a Strength Agent

Most children grow up within a family system whose members bear primary responsibility for the socialization of their children. Black church families consider children as their future and thus very important. Influenced by West African traditions, some congregations still follow the principle of communal parenting in which any adult may speak to a child's behavior and expect conformity. Although this practice is less mirrored within Black communities, it has not completely diminished in many churches. Most Black churches not only teach respect, collective responsibility, manners, and reciprocity but also place great emphasis on education. Social and religious activities (e.g., Sunday school, holiday speech recitations, and dramatic presentations) are designed specifically to enhance learning, memorization, self-concept, and effective communication. Many churches and community groups offer academic scholarships, tutoring, and mentoring services to the community. Teachers, counselors, and other helping professionals should obtain information about these services.

Implications for the Helping Context

Researchers have suggested that the spiritually inspired values and beliefs from religion or spirituality may manifest in helping situations with African American families (Boyd-Franklin, 1989; Locke, 1992; Richardson & June, 1997; Sanchez-Hucles, 1999). For example:

- Some church denominations have strict dress codes as well as regulations on, for example, dancing, smoking, drinking alcoholic beverages, attending parties, participating in sports events, and attending cinemas (Boyd-Franklin, 1989). Challenges may be noticed between the parental subsystem and their children, with grandparents, or among the parental subsystem if there is disagreement.
- Many denominations argue against premarital sex and by association the use of or discussion about birth control and contraceptives for teenagers or unmarried adults.
- Although attitudes about divorce and remarriage are changing, many churches discourage divorce and often influence couples' reconciliation without consideration of specific family dynamics.
- Many parents operate from a biblical parenting paradigm and view the use of corporal punishment as biblically responsible. They may cite scriptures such as "spare the rod; spoil the child," and they may be confused to learn that many counseling professionals consider this form of discipline abusive.
- Hierarchy is important in the church and mirrored in the home. Elders are to be respected, and the parental subsystem or its designate expects obedience from its children. Counselors should identify the power base within the family, which is not always the parental subsystem, and they should continually join with the family and seek to understand the place of the church. Because many African American children are socialized in homes with strong parental hierarchies, the exclusion of parents or their designates from the counseling process may, in some instances, negatively affect the establishment of rapport.
- Titles and values assigned to them are important in the Black church. This sentiment is also mirrored within many African American homes. Counselors who address older African Americans by their first names, especially in the presence of their adult children, run the risk of hampered rapport. Also, in some churches and communities, children do not address adults by their first names without also using a "handle," as in Sis Sheila or Miss Sheila or Bro Jones. A counselor who wants the child to refer to him or her by the first name, without verifying its appropriateness with the parents, may unknowingly confuse the child and cause the parents to question the moral values and upbringing of the counseling professional.
- The strong sense of faith in God may be expressed metaphorically using biblical phrases. The counselor may hear references

to God's will, listening for God's voice, and being under the attack of the enemy (the devil) "that can appear to the uninformed therapist to represent fatalism, a lack of internal control, or both" (Sanchez-Hucles, 1999, p. 13).

Conclusion

The Black church has historically provided and currently provides an invaluable resource for understanding and helping African American families. Many African American families rely on the Black church as an extended family for collective support. Counselors, educators, and other helping professionals will benefit by using this institution as a bridge in working with Black families.

References

Billingsley, A. (1968). *Black families in White America.* Englewood Cliffs, NJ: Prentice Hall.

Billingsley, A. (1992). *Climbing Jacob's ladder: The enduring legacy of African American families.* New York: Simon & Schuster.

Boyd-Franklin, N. (1989). *Black families in therapy: A multisystems approach.* New York: Guilford Press.

Brisbane, F. L., & Womble, M. (1985–1986). Treatment of Black alcoholics. *Alcoholism Treatment Quarterly, 2*(3/4).

DuBois, W. E. B. (1903). *The souls of Black folks: Essays and sketches.* Chicago: A. C. McClung.

Frazier, E. F. (1939). *The Black family in the United States.* Chicago: University of Chicago Press.

Frazier, E. F. (1964). *The Black church in America.* New York: Schocken Books.

Gutman, H. (1976). *The Black family in slavery and freedom: 1750–1925.* New York: Vintage Books.

Hawkins, D. (1993, December 30). Academics, politics, and the pulpit. *Black Issues in Higher Education,* pp. 14–17.

June, L. N. (Ed.). (1991). *The Black family: Past, present, and future: Perspectives of 16 Black Christian leaders.* Grand Rapids, MI: Zondervan.

Lester, J. (1968). *To be a slave.* New York: Dell.

Lincoln, C. E. (1990). *The Black church in the African American experience.* Durham, NC: Duke University Press.

Locke, D. C. (1992). *Increasing multicultural understanding: A comprehensive model.* Newbury Park, CA: Sage.

Madhubuti, H. R. (1994). *Claim earth: Race, rage, rape, redemption: Blacks seeking a culture of enlightened empowerment.* Chicago: Third World Press.

Nelsen, A., & Kusener-Nelsen, H. (1975). *Black church in the sixties*. Lexington: University of Kentucky Press.

Richardson, B. L., & June, L. N. (1997). Utilizing and maximizing the resources of the African American church: Strategies and tools for counseling professionals. In C. C. Lee (Ed.), *Multicultural issues in counseling: New approaches to diversity* (2nd ed., pp. 155–170). Alexandria, VA: American Counseling Association.

Rogers, R. (1971, October 25). *The early Black church*. Paper presented at Bowling Green State University, Bowling Green, KY.

Sanchez-Hucles, J. (1999). *The first session with African Americans: A step-by-step guide to the most crucial (and perhaps only) opportunity for effective change*. Retrieved from: http://www.josseybass.com/chapters/Sanchez.ch1.shtml

Washington, J. (1964). *Black religion*. Boston: Beacon Press.

■ ■ ■

PART **IV**

PULLING
THINGS
TOGETHER

7

IMPLICATIONS

Jo-Ann Lipford Sanders, PhD

Not to know is bad.
Not to want to know is worse.
Not to hope unthinkable.
Not to care unforgivable.

—Nigerian proverb

Historically, African American families have formed, survived, and benefited by using communal principles such as sharing, dependence, collective responsibility, interconnection, and reciprocity (Hill, 1998a) within an extended family context. The monograph began with a discussion of the effects of postmodernism on African American families. Changes in the function and structure of many African American families during this time have been attributed to economic opportunities, mobility, and various social and political advances. These changes have also fostered more isolated Black families that are physically distanced from their extended families as well as from large numbers of Black people. Researchers posit that African American families' continual use of communal principles suggest the power of these principles to transcend time and circumstance (Arnold, 1994; Boyd-Franklin, 1989; Hill, 1998b; Mosley-Howard & Burgan Evans, 2000; Neal-Barnett & Smith,

1997). Postmodern African American families use the communal principles in establishing new extended families comprised of friends, neighbors, other family groups, and church communities when they are unable to have the benefit of family-of-origin members. Counselors working with African American families may infuse the principles into their treatment plans and intervention methods (Hill, 1998b).

African American families, like other families, are neither all problem free nor all problem laden. They should be evaluated within the context of their individual experience. Counselors need to begin at the beginning—with a clearer understanding of universal commonalities and individual manifestations of behaviors that have been influenced by ethnicity, race, class, gender, and culture. This understanding may best be facilitated outside a paradigm of comparison with other groups (Helms & Cook, 1999).

Eighteen Suggestions to Help Counselors Begin Working With African American Families

1. Examine biases, stereotypes, and misconceptions. It is imperative for counselors, teachers, and all mental health providers to examine themselves in respect to biases, stereotypes, and misconceptions about African American culture. I know of no individual who is totally value-free. A mental health provider's unexamined values and assumptions may impede the counseling process. Rather than label the dynamics of a difficult counseling session as resistance on the part of the African American family, examine where or how your own lack of knowledge—that accounts for unchallenged biases, stereotypes, and misconceptions—may in fact be an active third party in the counseling process. Hardy and Laszloffy (1992) stated that a lack of preparedness to work with and understand African American families makes "it difficult to distinguish between behavior that is detrimental to family health and that which is racially sanctioned" (p. 367).

2. Build the rapport that is very important for effective counseling practice. A key aspect of effective counseling is the establishment of rapport. Historically, African American people have not voluntarily participated in traditional counseling services. Often the majority of counseling professionals have been individuals of the dominant culture whose training and practice supported Western socialization. One of the most important dimensions of establishing rapport with Black families is to help them feel that they are being heard. Uncritically examine the family dynamics to understand the power structure. Seek to join with the family by providing respect for its senior members or those designated as power persons. Listen and consider life experiences that have been influenced by discrimination and racism. When funneled through a prism of individualism and internal locus of control, these experiences may sound like helplessness, excuses, blaming, and dependency. Rapport building is enhanced when counselors take the time to "hear the story" of the family. Families that have experienced oppression are often very sensitized to (a) not being heard, (b) feeling blamed, and (c) having to explain things that are significant in their lives to people they feel do not have a frame of reference. Good counseling skills become great counseling skills in establishing rapport when effectively used.

3. To understand African American families, begin with the African historical experience as a frame of reference. When evaluating African American families, much effort has been put into a comparison model with middle-class European Americans. Many counselors have limited knowledge about the evolution, adaptive structures, and functions of various African and African American family types. Although the postmodern African American family mirrors European American families, many familial patterns of African culture also provide a backdrop of thought in such areas as discipline practices, respect for adults, community responsibility, and spirituality.

4. Become knowledgeable about how various Black people are experiencing sociopolitical and cultural dimensions. This may be facilitated by reading literature concentrated on African Americans and their families. To work with African American families, counselors should embrace a multidisciplinary focus on their past and current experiences. Additionally, counselors should be knowledgeable about the current status of race relations and engage the client in discourse addressing the possible effects of discrimination if needed. Not all problems reflect intrapsychic conflicts; many also are sociopsychological conflicts relating to the interaction between daily oppressive systems and the client's perception (White & Parham, 1990).

5. Find out how the particular African American family defines culture and its influence. Culture is more than dress,

holidays, movements, and/or language. It involves the way in which
an individual makes sense of the world. Ask the client questions
that will give you information to determine the worldview of the
family. How do race, class, ethnicity, and gender differences influence the family's worldview? Has the family been influenced by
"isms"? What is the family's cultural interpretation of "family secrets"? How is mental illness and mental health defined within this
family? Does the definition seem appropriate or inappropriate given
the family's cultural interpretations? What is the racial identity level
of the person who wields the most power in the family? This information will be primary in making an assessment about the worldview
that is guiding the family unit.

**6. Explore the role that spirituality or religion plays in
the family's life.** Seek to understand the principles taken from
African spirituality and religion. How might they manifest in the
family's daily life? Often these principles are useful in assisting clients in reframing a problem. Is prayer or meditation useful? Notice
how continual references to God or a higher power helping or providing a way out of distress may be misconstrued as signs of helplessness. Are there significant spiritual leaders who may assist your
efforts (Helms & Cook, 1999)?

**7. Expand the lens that is used to view the world beyond
a purely nuclear family context.** The overemphasis on "all posi-
tives" associated with a traditional nuclear family context has contributed to other systems being labeled as deficient. When working
with African American families, counselors will notice various functional structures. Although there are many female-headed African
American homes, there are often familial others providing external
supports. Here is a wonderful opportunity to challenge traditional
thinking about the dynamics of a successful home. There are many
grandmothers who have reorganized their lives to take care of grandchildren. There are many single Black fathers who are also parenting.
Very often these family units have the assistance of community
groups, churches, and fictive kin, and are highly functional. The
African proverb "a person is a person through other persons" en-
capsulates the community perspective of many African American
family structures (Burton & Jayakody, 2001; Hill, 1998a, 1998b).

8. Put African American families in a truer context. Challenge the stereotype suggesting that these families are without a
father, are on welfare, are thriftless, matrifocal, and overpopulated

with illegitimate children. Although African American families are not problem free, not all of their problems have a cause-and-effect relationship with the single-female-headed family structures. Notice how individuals within this family structure adapt to and redefine their family roles. Help the clients see how these adaptive measures are examples of resiliency and strength. Guide them in reconstructing these strengths in other situations.

9. Understand how the specific family you are working with is organized. Extended families are very common in African American communities. In the first or second session, find out how the family operates. Who wields significant power relating to parenting? To money? To power? To decision making? How is power defined within this structure? Are there individuals who do not physically live in the household but whose "presence" is considered in household decisions? How many constellations does this family represent? Find out what roles are played by family members, noticing that roles are often assigned according to necessity rather than custom. Be careful not to assume automatically that a child engaging in duties historically defined as adult (and often identified in the literature as a "parentified" child) has equal adult power or is being robbed of a childhood. In many African American families adults are respected and revered because of their status, sometimes regardless of their actual duties. Evaluate each family individually.

10. Broaden your perspectives to include consideration that learning about diversity is a lifelong process, that there are no shortcuts or quick fixes. Counselors will best serve African American consumers by continual training in culturally responsive courses. We believe that all counselors must have or receive training in the fundamental principles of multicultural counseling. The Association for Multicultural Counseling and Development has recommended specific multicultural counseling competencies for counselors working with clients from culturally diverse backgrounds (Arrendondo et al., 1996).

11. Develop ways to ask questions about the influences of race in the lives of these families. As long as society is race conscious, there is the probability that racism and various forms of oppression also exist and that racism and some forms of oppression may touch the lives of African American families. Facilitate an environment of unconditional positive regard in which issues of race, class, gender, and ethnicity may be normatively discussed. Counselors, teachers, and other helping professionals need to help many African American families recognize and confront oppression and racism and their residuals as impacting on worldview. A career issue, for example, might be associated with gender and race.

12. Acknowledge heterogeneity and challenge any notion of sameness for all Black people that is based on their skin color. When working with African American families, counselors need to develop an understanding of the relevance of heterogeneity. Many African American scholars articulate various aspects of the Black experience, including Black psychology (White & Parham, 1990), feminism (Collins, 1991), child discipline (Bradley, 1998), family dynamics (Boyd-Franklin, 1989; Jones, 1991), children (Spencer, Brookins, & Allen, 1985), couples (Hopson & Hopson, 1994), and women (Pack-Brown, Whittington-Clark, & Parker, 1998). These writings and research must be included within traditional training programs. Counselors have to desire a fundamental change in both thinking and attitude. Many Black people born outside the United States who do not self-identify as African American may be touched by racism because of their skin color. It is important to note they will generally report a different perspective about race dynamics and may be unable to fully understand the sentiments of African Americans or their personal feelings of exclusion and isolation. Often because they cannot understand racism, they have a difficult time articulating their feelings about how racism affects their lives. Counselors who are familiar with oppression could be useful in helping these clients understand and articulate their feelings.

13. Listen for and allow the family to identify its strengths. Help families by pointing out areas of resiliency and adaptive skills as strengths. Build your helping plan around each family's strengths. In addition, teach skills that will be useful in navigating social obstacles. The humorous activities of Africans were historically viewed as childish; however, humor has been a source of strength in the midst of oppression for many cultures. Notice if your treatment is devoid of humor or requires that Black people give up their use of humor, laughing, and play.

14. Make sure your facilities, schools, and offices are welcoming to African American families. Do your staff and environment (e.g., pictures, magazines) reflect inclusion?

15. Develop a resource bank of helpers and help sites. There are many organizations within various African American communities that offer self-help. Are you aware of the resources available in the area, such as churches, temples and community centers? Have you developed any connection with local ministers? With sororities, fraternities, social clubs? Are you familiar with rites of passage programs and other programs designed specifically within African American communities? Ally with these groups as they can provide mentors as well as guest speakers for schools, and they can be trained as possible group cofacilitators.

16. Stop searching for THE intervention strategy that works for African American people. Bucher (1999, p. 20) called the desire to seek hurried responses to complex issues the McDonaldization of our society. Multisystems family therapy has been suggested as an effective means to use with Black families (Boyd-Franklin, 1989; Tucker, 1999). Group therapy has proven successful with children and women (Jordan, 1997; Pack-Brown, Whittington-Clark, & Parker, 1998) as well as men (Lee, 1991, 1993; Lee & Bailey, 1997; Wynn, 1992), especially when issues of race, gender, and oppression are included in the discussions and curriculum.

17. Seek to understand how ethnicity, culture, social class, and gender affect the development of identity in African American children. Counselors often learn about developmental issues with Black children and adolescents without acknowledging the significant impact of environmental variables. The search for identity can be difficult for all children. African American children and indeed all children of color have added pressures in developing a healthy sense of self in a society of race hierarchy. Often Black children exhibit this intrapsychic struggle in socially significant ways. Scholars investigating Black children have noted the impact of racism and oppression on the developmental lives of Black children in social anxiety (Neal-Barnett & Smith, 1997); in hiding their intelligence or desire for learning so as not to appear to be "actin' White," thus further alienating them from other Black adolescents; and in depressive and acting-out behaviors (Leonard, Lee, & Koselica, 1999; Tucker, 1999). Further, many other Black children search for ways to make sense of the world by reinventing themselves, as may be seen in their subcultural language and dress. Counselors need to listen for instances when this struggle is prevalent. One college student commented that

To be a Black man in this society is hard, but not that hard that I shouldn't push to make my goals come true...it all started when I found out I was going to a college...to play ball. I got that chance...everyone was proud of their son, as well as their boy for taking the chance to better his self in today's cruel world. Besides the man using me to win him a championship in basketball, everyone I knew wanted me to get them out of the hood with me. Of course I'm going to help my boys that I grew up with. This was my ace boon koons...a small problem arose when I came home after the first year ended. Everything I said or did, I was acting White or I was a gay guy. Everything that I said was wrong, because they said that I was trying to be better than them...the situation was getting on my nerve because I could not understand why my peoples were dogging me out because I was in school...in class one day we were talking...helped me understand what I was going through...you got to live with it or kill yourself. I know that I got things to achieve for my two sons and I, so don't look for my funeral arrangements yet. (Bucher, 1999, p. 27)

18. Develop culturally responsive family programs. Locke (1997) emphasized the following considerations in developing and structuring programs to be culturally responsive to African American families:

- *Family centeredness.* Family-centered practice is an approach to the delivery of services that focuses on the entire family system rather than on identified individuals, with the ultimate aim of supporting families, keeping children safe, and preserving families whenever possible. Family centeredness is an essential consideration in developing culturally responsive programs for African American families.
- *Location of program.* Culturally responsive programs are community based, easily accessible, and located in communities and neighborhoods in which families live. For example, programs might be located in churches, schools, day care centers, libraries, hospitals, nonprofit agencies, community recreation centers, boys and girls clubs, YMCAs.
- *Consumer involvement.* Consumers are partners in the development, maintenance, and functioning of culturally responsive programs. Participation and involvement in all levels of the organization is encouraged and valued. Consumer representation is reflected in board membership, administrative and policy development, program development, implementation and evaluation, new program development, and staffing decisions.

- *Staffing.* Professionals, paraprofessionals, and volunteers staff culturally responsive programs, and staff are preferably residents in the immediate community. All staff members have a personal commitment to delivering culturally relevant services, and they receive basic and ongoing training in self-awareness and cultural issues.
- *Program goals.* Among other programmatic goals, culturally responsive programs strive to support families, empower families for independence and self-sufficiency, and seek to preserve cultural and ethnic identity.
- *Program services.* Programmatic and intervention strategies are consistent with the values, beliefs, and behaviors of consumers and might include such culturally relevant factors as bilingual services, culturally based assessment approaches, outreach services, family survival resources, and natural helping systems.
- *Continuum of services.* Culturally responsive programs recognize that some families need more holistic services than tend to be typically offered at specialized agencies. Therefore, assessments are multidimensional and attempt comprehensively to identify strengths and needs of participating families. Culturally responsive agencies tend to be well connected to other community resources and provide linkages (referral and advocacy) to other community agencies in an effort to serve families more holistically.
- *Research and program evaluation.* Research and program evaluation is conducted in a way that is culturally sensitive by selecting research methodologies and instruments that are not biased against a particular cultural group. Research and evaluation include agency staff in the design and conduct of research. Findings are used to redefine existing programs and develop new programs.

Not all African American families internalize oppression in the same way. Not all African American families even acknowledge the residual effects of oppression. Although racism does not guide every facet of African American families, its effects are nonetheless far reaching. Culturally responsive counseling with African American families should foster an environment in which the subject of oppression may be considered. Preconceived notions about African Americans and their culture, whether birthed in historical accounts or familial socialization, often inhibit effective counseling. The use of a strength-resiliency approach in which the African

American family is an active participant in identifying and defining adaptive strategies is most useful. The literature suggests that strategies that are "culturally different" or unconventional may in fact be very adaptive (Boyd-Franklin, 1989; Bradley, 1998; Burton & Jayakody, 2001; Hill, 1998a, 1998b).

References

Arnold, M. S. (1994). Exploding the myths: African American families at promise. In S. Lubbeck & E. Swadener (Eds.), *Children and families at promise.* Albany: State University of New York Press.

Arredondo, P., Toporek, R., Brown, S. P., Jones, J., Locke, D. C., Sanchez, J., & Stadler, H. (January, 1996). *Operationalization of the multicultural counseling competencies.* Alexandria, VA: Association for Multicultural Counseling and Development, American Counseling Association.

Boyd-Franklin, N. (1989). *Black families in therapy: A multisystems approach.* New York: Guilford Press.

Bradley, C. (1998). Child rearing in African American families: A study of disciplinary methods used by African American parents. *Journal of Multicultural Counseling and Development, 26,* 273–281.

Bucher, R. D. (1999). *Diversity consciousness: Opening our minds to people, cultures, and opportunities.* Upper Saddle River, NJ: Prentice Hall.

Burton, L. M., & Jayakody, R. (2001). Rethinking family structure and single parenthood: Implications for future studies of African American families and children. In A. Thornton (Ed.), *The well-being of children and families: Research and data needs* (pp. 127–153). Ann Arbor: University of Michigan Press.

Collins, P. H. (1991). *Black feminist thought: Knowledge consciousness and the politics of empowerment.* New York: Routledge.

Hardy, K. V., & Laszloffy, T. A. (1992). Training racially sensitive family therapists: Context, content, and contact. *Families in Society: The Journal of Contemporary Human Services,* 364–370.

Helms, J. E., & Cook, D. A. (1999). *Using race and culture in counseling and psychotherapy: Theory and process.* Needham Heights, MA: Allyn & Bacon.

Hill, R. B. (1998a). Enhancing the resilience of African American families. *Journal of Human Behavior in the Social Environment, 1*(2–3). 49–61.

Hill, R. B. (1998b). Understanding Black family functioning: A holistic perspective. *Journal of Comparative Family Studies, 29*(1), 15–25.

Hopson, D. S., & Hopson, D. P. (1994). *Friends, lovers, and soul mates: A guide to better relationships between Black men and women.* New York: Simon and Schuster.

Jones, F. L. (Ed.). (1991). *Black psychology* (3rd ed.). Berkeley, CA: Cobb & Henry.

Jordan, J. M. (1997). Counseling African American women from a cultural sensitivity perspective. In C. C. Lee (Ed.), *Multicultural issues in counseling: New approaches to diversity* (2nd ed., pp. 109–121). Alexandria, VA: American Counseling Association.

Lee, C. C. (1991). Counseling African Americans: From theory to practice. In R. L. Jones (Ed.), *Black psychology* (3rd ed., pp. 559–576). Berkeley, CA: Cobb & Henry.

Lee, C. C. (1993). Psychology and African Americans: New perspectives for the 1990s. In E. R. Myers (Ed.), *Challenges of a changing America: Perspectives on immigration and multiculturalism in the United States* (pp. 57–64). San Francisco: Austin & Winfield.

Lee, C. C., & Bailey, D. F. (1997). Counseling African American male youth and men. In C. C. Lee (Ed.), *Multicultural issues in counseling: New approaches to diversity* (2nd ed., pp. 123–154). Alexandria, VA: American Counseling Association.

Leonard, S., Lee, C., & Koselica, M. S. (1999) Counseling African American male youth. In A. M. Horne & M. S. Koselica (Eds.), *Handbook of counseling boys and adolescent males: A practitioner's guide* (pp. 75–86). Thousand Oaks, CA: Sage.

Locke, D. C. (1997, February 14). *Culturally responsive family programs.* Presented at the National Convention of the American Counseling Association.

Mosley-Howard, G. S., & Burgan Evans, C. (2000). Relationships and contemporary experiences of the African American family: An ethnographic case study. *Journal of Black Studies, 30*(3), 428–452.

Neal-Barnett, A., & Smith, J. (1997). African Americans. In S. Friedman (Ed.), *Cultural issues in the treatment of anxiety* (pp. 154–174). New York: Guilford Press.

Pack-Brown, S. P., Whittington-Clark, L. E., & Parker, W. M. (1998). *Images of me: A guide to group work with African American women.* Boston: Allyn & Bacon.

Spencer, M. B., Brookins, G. L., & Allen, W. R. (Eds.). (1985). *Beginnings: The social and affective development of Black children.* Hillsdale, NJ: Erlbaum.

Tucker, C. M. (1999). *African American children: A self-empowerment approach to modifying behavior problems and preventing academic failure.* Boston: Allyn & Bacon.

White, J. L., & Parham, T. A. (1990). *The psychology of Blacks: An African American perspective* (2nd ed.). Englewood Cliffs, NJ: Prentice Hall.

Wynn, M. (1992). *Empowering African American males to succeed: A 10-step approach for parents and teachers.* South Pasadena, CA: Rising Sun.

■ ■ ■